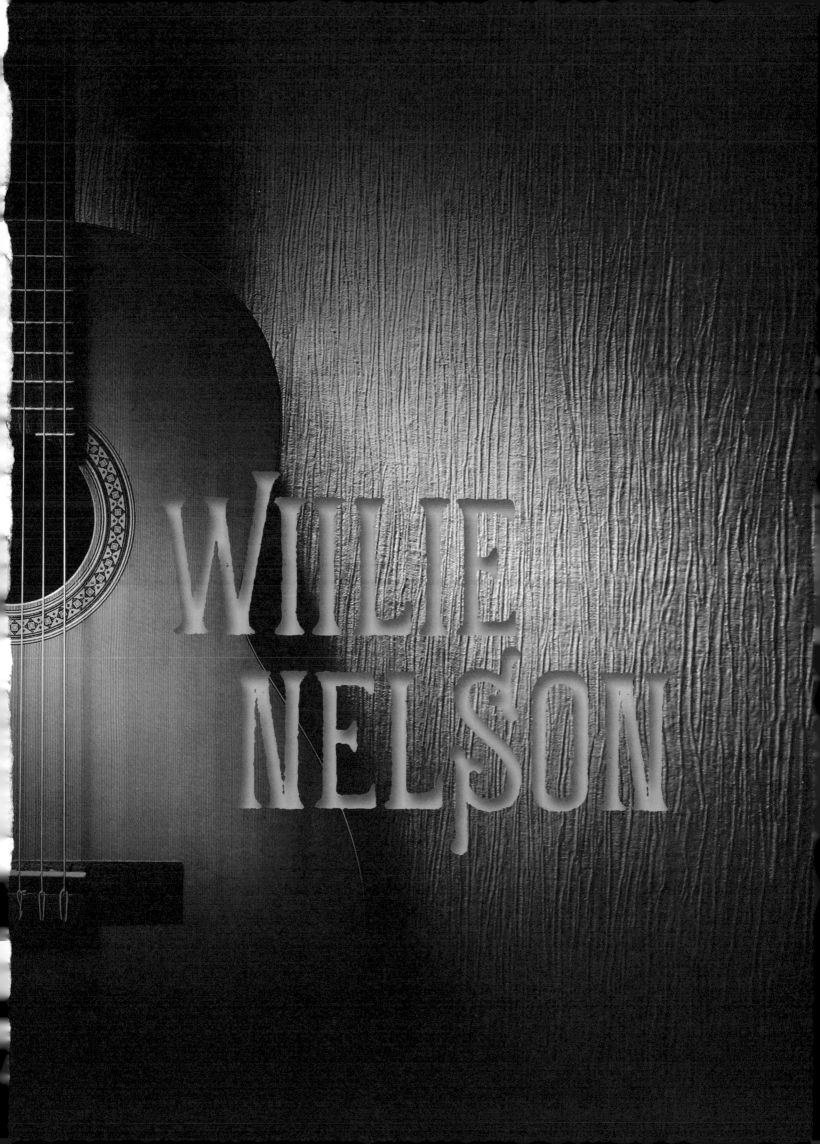

STERLING
New York

An Imprint of Sterling Publishing Co., Inc.
1166 Avenue of the Americas
New York, NY 10036

ISBN 978-1-4549-2619-1

Distributed in Canada by Sterling Publishing Co., Inc.
c/o Canadian Manda Group, 664 Annette Street
Toronto, Ontario, Canada M6S 2C8
Distributed in the United Kingdom by GMC Distribution Services
Castle Place, 166 High Street, Lewes, East Sussex, England BN7 1XU
Distributed in Australia by NewSouth Books
45 Beach Street, Coogee, NSW 2034, Australia

For information about custom editions, special sales, and premium and corporate purchases, please contact
Sterling Special Sales at 800-805-5489 or
specialsales@sterlingpublishing.com

Manufactured in China

1 2 3 4 5 6 7 8 9 10

www.sterlingpublishing.com

Design by Essential Works

Picture Credits—See page 208

ANDREW VAUGHAN

WILLIE NELSON

★ AMERICAN ICON ★

STERLING
New York

CONTENTS

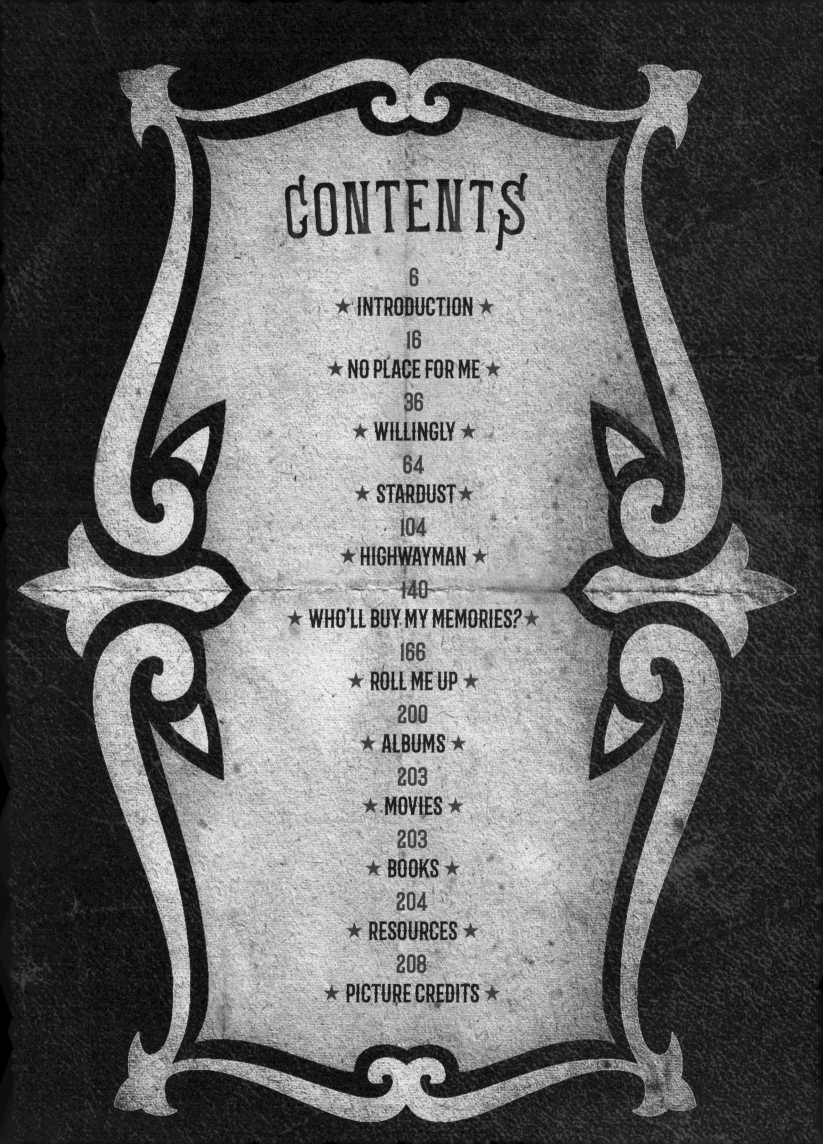

Introduction

OPPOSITE

Willie Nelson in 1975 at an in-store record promotion in Atlanta, Georgia.

L ondon, England, 1988. It was the annual Easter-time International Festival of Country Music, and Willie Nelson and his band were headlining. I was there, a novice journalist reporting on the festival for BBC Radio. Traditional country music had a strong enough following in the UK in the 1980s for Wembley Arena to be packed to the rafters with British and European country fans. Many of the audience were decked out in Western attire, resembling a vast Waylon Jennings and Willie Nelson lookalike contest.

New to the festival setup, I wandered from the sanctity of the press area and somehow turned up backstage, inadvertently backing into the imposing Paul English, Nelson's longtime drummer and bodyguard. English's no-nonsense stare was enough to petrify me, but the tension was lifted when a calm voice said, "Hi. I'm Willie Nelson, how you doing?" English grinned and walked away, and Willie and I chit-chatted for a minute or two. He had recognized my nerves, rescued me from making an ass of myself, and shown himself to be a man of modesty, charm, and empathy. I was too nervous to recall what the country music legend said to me in those short exchanges, but it ended with him saying he had to go get ready to "sing a few songs and entertain the folks."

And that's what he has been doing since the 1950s, singing a few songs and entertaining the world.

It's easy to look at Willie Nelson's sixty years of achievements and recognize him as a genuine hero of the people, a true artist and spokesman for his times, and indeed an icon of American popular culture.

Willie's successes are truly remarkable. A struggling songwriter whose inner faith refused to allow himself be eaten up by the uncaring music business in Nashville, he discovered the artist inside himself in the 1970s and went from the neatly coiffed and suited writer of good songs for others to the long-haired star of a new brand of music—all in the space of a few short months.

Willie Nelson has had a sixty-year music career, released over 150 albums, starred in a number of well-respected Hollywood movies, written a few best-selling books, and received practically every honor there is, save perhaps a knighthood from the queen of England!

At the time of this writing, in the last five years alone he delivered ten new album releases, performed at Farm Aid annually, played over 150 concerts each year, received his fifth-degree black belt in Gong Kwon Yusol, and wrote a best-seller.

He debuted once again at #1 on Billboard's country album chart with *Django and Jimmie*, recorded with his old friend Merle Haggard, shortly before the latter's death in April 2016. In November 2015, he became the first country

music singer to be awarded the esteemed Library of Congress Gershwin Prize for Popular Song, and then aptly recorded an album of Gershwin tunes that took him to the top of the jazz charts.

In his eighty-plus years there have been some terrible lows as well as superb highs. His childhood was tough; he was raised by grandparents after he and his sister were abandoned by their married-too-young parents. He's been through three failed marriages and the loss of almost everything he owned at the hands of the tax authorities, and, devastatingly, had to be given the news of his son Billy's suicide. Imbued with more than a normal share of empathy, Nelson has stood up for minorities, been an avid campaigner for the environment and for those less fortunate than himself, and consistently challenged the government on its marijuana laws. He's been arrested numerous times, yet he never gave up speaking his mind on issues that matter. He lives on a philosophy of karma and positive thinking, mixed with a little weed, golf, and, of course, music—and has remained a hero to almost everyone in his native Texas, millions in America, and many more around the world.

But who is Willie Nelson? His great friend Johnny Cash said Willie was a hard man to get to know, writing in 1997 that Nelson "keeps his inner thoughts for himself and his songs. He just doesn't talk much at all, in fact. When he does, what he says is usually very perceptive and precise. He has a beautiful sense of irony and a true appreciation for the absurd. I really like him."

Nelson's characteristic mix of toughness and kindness—blended with a gypsy heart and a maverick spirit—initially developed in small town Texas in the 1930s. As he told *Texas Monthly* in December 1999, all he really wanted do was grow up to be cowboy, "I started out watching Gene Autry and Roy Rogers every Saturday on the movie screen in Hillsboro. I knew what I wanted to do: I wanted to be a singing cowboy, ride my horse, play my guitar, and shoot my gun. So here we are."

Autry, cowboy star of the 1940s on radio, records, TV, and the movie screen, had a significant impact on the youth of post-Depression America. Not only was he the good guy in his movies, radio, and TV shows, but he developed a code to live by, ten moral rules that he called the Cowboy Code:

Gene Autry's
COWBOY CODE

1. The Cowboy must never shoot first, hit a smaller man, or take unfair advantage.

2. He must never go back on his word, or a trust confided in him.

3. He must always tell the truth.

4. He must be gentle with children, the elderly, and animals.

5. He must not advocate or possess racially or religiously intolerant ideas.

6. He must help people in distress.

7. He must be a good worker.

8. He must keep himself clean in thought, speech, action, and personal habits.

9. He must respect women, parents, and his nation's laws.

10. The Cowboy is a patriot.

Nelson, for me, took Autry's code to heart, and he has lived the words of his hero for most of his long life.

Woody Harrelson, a neighbor of Nelson's in Hawaii, recently told *Rolling Stone* magazine's Patrick Doyle about his admiration for Nelson's kindness: "There's some freakin' nut cases that come by his house on the regular. These are people I wouldn't have over a second time. And he just treats them great, and he'll give jobs

OPPOSITE

Always a passionate
advocate of law reform
regarding marijuana, Willie
relaxes at his home in Texas.

to people who don't have money—you know, 'Sweep this up.' He leads with his heart, and it's a beautiful thing to behold."

At Nelson's televised seventieth birthday concert, he was introduced onstage by former president Bill Clinton, in a mini exchange that perfectly illustrated Nelson's unassuming humility and care for others, as well as his ever-present sense of humor.

Clinton told a special Nelson story that very few people knew. "The national stock-car drivers were meeting on the back lawn of the White House, and Willie Nelson was there to entertain them. There was a young boy in the crowd who was dying of cancer. He was sixteen years old. He's already had one of his arms amputated. He was bald from chemotherapy. And Willie Nelson went out in the crowd and got that kid and brought him up on the stage and sat him on a stool for the entire concert. It was never in the press, it wasn't on television. Nobody ever knew it. He did it because that's who he is."

In the segregated America of the 1960s, Nelson gave an African American singer, Charley Pride, an opening spot on his tour. When a crowd looked like they were being hostile to Pride, Nelson grabbed Charley and kissed him full on the lips. That may not seem exceptional now, but fifty years ago in a segregated nightclub in Texas, that was the action of a man who cared and who dared to do the right thing. Ever since, Nelson has remained a man of the people.

He's been outspoken against what he feels are unnecessary and unproductive marijuana laws since the early 1970s. From that came his passion for the hemp industry and its benefit to agriculture in the United States.

In 1985, when thousands of America's farmers were suffering financially, Nelson, along with fellow singers John Mellencamp and Neil Young, launched Farm Aid with a benefit concert to raise money for farmers facing foreclosure. The event has since been staged annually, with a rotating roster of guest artists alongside the founders. As recognition, in 2011, Nelson was inducted into the National Agricultural Hall of Fame. Over his career Willie has supported many other benefit gigs and charitable organizations, and even started a biodiesel fuel company, BioWillie.

Willie Nelson does things his own way. Despite numerous setbacks in the early years of his music career, he never stopped pursuing his passions. He was determined to be an artist and an entertainer. It took a very long time, and Nelson was close to giving up on several occasions. If he couldn't get record companies to see his appeal, he'd write tunes for others—and he did. He wrote hit songs like "Hello Walls" for Faron Young and the all-time classic "Crazy" for Patsy Cline. But Willie's voice was "off" his detractors said, his phrasing wrong to be a vocal artist in his own right.

The guitar genius and top producer Chet Atkins was one of the first to recognize Nelson's unique quality and tried to make him a star, although Nelson and the Nashville factory system just didn't gel. As he was continually being told, his style didn't fit with the times. His songs did, for sure, but his hesitant, almost talking vocals were unlike any other successful country singer at the time. But money from songwriting meant Willie could retain some musical independence until the right opportunity arose.

Things finally began to happen in 1972, when he was signed to rock-and-soul label Atlantic's new Nashville division. His debut for Atlantic, *Shotgun Willie*, produced by the legendary soul men Arif Mardin and Jerry Wexler, saw a more adventurous but relaxed Willie Nelson. He was finding his voice. At the same time, some of his country music cohorts, inspired by the freedoms and riches enjoyed by their rock-and-roll cousins, wanted to change the way Nashville did business— or at least find a way of having more control. Fellow maverick and good friend Waylon Jennings fought the system from the inside, while Nelson moved to Texas to find his way. Both men found fame and musical glory with the all-conquering outlaw country movement of the early '70s, which saw country music's rebels grow beards, wear their hair long, and fuse delightfully with hippie-style rock-and-roll.

Nelson had stood firm, stuck to his principles, and, after many years, come out on top. And it would have been easy, now that he had achieved what he'd been dreaming of for so long, to play it safe. But that wasn't the Nelson way. He might have been pigeonholed as a country artist, but Nelson loved all kinds of music, especially jazz, swing, and pop standards. So, just as he was at the top of the country music game, in 1978 he recorded an album of songs drawn from the great American songbook, naming it for his favorite Hoagy Carmichael song, "Stardust." The record company tried to dissuade him from the project, Nelson disagreed, and the album became his biggest selling ever, crossing over into markets that no country act had ever reached before.

Success has never changed Willie much—he's played the same guitar, nicknamed "Trigger," since 1969—and in his consistency and persistence in making music that he loves, he has never followed any kind of commercial fashion. For that as much as anything else, when Willie saw everything taken from him in 1991 by the IRS to pay taxes, he found a lot of love forthcoming from both his industry and the American public. His subsequent tours and 1992 album release, *The IRS Tapes*, raised enough money to keep the tax man happy and enable Willie to start over again.

Confident in his own abilities, Willie Nelson didn't hesitate when asked to try his hand as an actor. He has appeared in more than thirty films and TV dramas, even starring in a couple, most notably 1980's *Honeysuckle Rose* and *Barbarosa* in 1982.

Willie Nelson and his band, the Family, still travel the nation, playing concerts for at least half the year in a custom-made tour bus. Folks pose with the bus when it's parked, and sometimes Willie climbs down to pose with them, too. He's never been remote from his fans, always coming across as approachable, honest, and witty.

When Willie Nelson saved his old church in his hometown of Abbott, Texas, it was clear that his roots still mattered. From singing duets with pop starts like Julio Iglesias, to working with rock-and-roll legends like Bob Dylan and Neil Young or country greats like Johnny Cash and Waylon Jennings—or indeed acting on screen alongside Hollywood superstars like Robert Redford—Willie Nelson has never forgotten where he comes from. And it was music and his skills as an entertainer that took him from picking cotton in Texas to smoking weed on the roof of the White House.

As he told Aaron Jensen on Biography.com in 2015, "When I was about eleven or twelve years old, I had been working in the field, picking cotton, baling hay, for a couple of bucks a day. And then I got this job in this Bohemian polka band one night, and I made eight dollars the first night, just playing music, doing my best to keep up with the boys. And I said to myself, 'Well, here we go. This is success.' And I've just been that way ever since."

—ANDREW VAUGHAN, DECEMBER 2016

OPPOSITE

Willie Nelson as an outlaw in the title role of the western movie *Barbarosa,* 1982.

FOLLOWING SPREAD

On stage during the 2009 Farm Aid benefit at the Verizon Wireless Amphitheater, St. Louis, Missouri, October, 2009.

1

1933 ✴ 1955

No Place for Me

"I've always felt like Abbott was a special place. It was the perfect place for me to grow up because it was a small town and because everybody knew everybody. Everybody there was friends or family or worked together or went to school together. There was something real positive about that." So said Willie Nelson, as he spoke with *Texas Monthly*'s Evan Smith in December 2005.

Lessons learned growing up in Texas—and small-town Texas in particular—have remained with Willie Nelson throughout the highs and lows of his long music career. What is more, Willie has backed up a lifelong loyalty to his hometown in real ways. He's helped keep Abbott a thriving community, despite (with a population of little over 300) it being barely larger than it was in the 1930s, when he and his family were struggling through the Great Depression.

Three stories illustrate the genuine affection Nelson holds for Abbott. In the middle of winter 1993, the town's historic courthouse caught on fire, burning to the ground. When Willie heard about the disaster, he headed to Abbott and put on a fundraising concert. Inviting fellow artists to take part, he raised enough cash to have the court premises rebuilt. In 2006, he learned that the church he attended as a boy, Abbott United Methodist Church, was in financial ruin due to declining membership. With his older sister Bobbie, Willie stepped in and purchased the church before it could be pulled down. And shortly after that, he similarly saved the town's general store, Abbott Cash Grocery & Market, where his family had shopped when he was growing up. Now, in addition to groceries, you can buy vintage T-shirts and posters from Willie Nelson concerts, and every cent helps keep the store and church operating, as well as contributing to scholarships for students at Abbott High School.

PREVIOUS PAGES

Willie Nelson in a typical publicity shot from early in his recording career.

GROWING UP

When Willie Nelson was born on April 29, 1933, the town of Abbott was facing a battle for survival like most small towns across America. A small hill country settlement in North Central Texas, Abbott had grown steadily since its beginnings as a railroad town some fifty years earlier. In 1920, it had prospered enough to warrant having a highway built through the middle of town, but the road would receive far less traffic than anticipated. By 1933, the year Willie Nelson was born, the road was eerily quiet and trains had to be flagged down for them to stop. It was the Great Depression and, like most of Texas, Abbott was hit hard.

Texas had been economically strong through the first couple of decades of the twentieth century, but financial progress came to a halt on October 29, 1929, the infamous "Black Tuesday," when the value of millions of shares on Wall Street plummeted. The Dow Jones Industrial Average dropped, and billions of dollars were lost overnight. In just three years stocks became worth just one-fifth of their pre-crash value. Initially Texas's booming oil industry and strong farming communities weathered the financial storms pretty well, but by the early 1930s it was clear that the state—like the rest of America—was in for a rough ride.

If that wasn't a challenging enough environment to be born into, when Willie was only six months old his mother, Myrtle, left Abbott for Portland, Oregon, leaving Willie and his older sister, Bobbie, with their father, Ira. Myrtle and Ira had been married at just sixteen years of age. Ira, who came from English and Irish stock, loved music and was a decent fiddle player, but was content to just play dances around the local area. Myrtle's family were was known for their love

BELOW

A spectacular panoramic view of the booming oilfields in Texas, as they appeared in the first half of the twentieth century.

ABOVE

Willie and his older sister,
Bobbie Lee Nelson, teenage
siblings in 1949. Bobbie
was born on New Year's
Day 1931, and Willie two
years later, in April 1933.

of music (and illicit moonshine liquor!), and, unlike her husband, the young bride was filled with a wanderlust and sense of adventure that would keep her on the move.

Willie's father soon found himself a new wife, and he also moved away from Abbott, leaving the Nelson children to be raised by their paternal grandparents, Alfred and Nancy, or, as Bobbie and Willie called them, Mama and Daddy.

Despite the loss of their natural parents, the children were raised with love and care by the Nelson grandparents, and while money was always an issue, they were well looked after. Their father attempted to stay in touch with Willie and Bobbie, but Alfred was very protective of the children, although he did allow Ira to visit his home on occasion.

The siblings were raised in a home that valued its Christian tradition, and with their grandmother being musical director for the local Methodist Church, they were immersed in music from early on. The family sang together, learned songs together, and even wrote tunes as a family. Both Bobbie and Willie picked up, either via nature or nurture, a raw talent for music that would direct their lives and careers over the next seven decades. When Willie was just six years old his grandfather bought him a cheap guitar from the Sears, Roebuck mail-order catalog, and the youngster displayed an immediate affinity with the instrument.

"WHEN I WAS A KID I USED TO PLAY THE MANDOLIN – FOOL WITH IT A LOT, AND THE BANJO, AND EVERYTHING THAT HAD STRINGS ON IT … BUT I NEVER REALLY TRIED TO GET GOOD ON ANYTHING OTHER THAN A GUITAR." —WILLIE NELSON

"I started out with a thumb pick," Willie told *Frets* magazine in December 1984, "because that was what my grandparents used, so I was taught that way. But later on I began to hear players like Eldon Shamblin [of Bob Wills and the Texas Playboys], and they used a straight pick. So I changed because that music was more what I wanted to play. When I was a kid I used to play the mandolin—fool with it a lot, and the banjo, and everything that had strings on it. I usually could get some sort of sound out of them. But I never really tried to get good on anything other than a guitar."

Willie Nelson's birth parents may have left the town of Abbott, but his grandparents were rooted in the fabric of the small town and made sure that the kids also appreciated the value of a close, supportive farming community. As for preparing him for the outside world, Abbott, according to Nelson, was simply a microcosm of the United States. He told Evan Smith of *Texas Monthly* in December 2005 that "Abbott was a little bitty picture of the whole world. You had nice people, you had assholes, and you learned to live with them, and like them, and work with them. I thought it was a good education growing up there."

Hank Williams

Hank Williams was country music's greatest ever superstar, and a major influence on Willie Nelson. He was just twenty-nine years old when he died on the backseat of his '52 Cadillac, as his driver took him from Knoxville Tennessee to a concert date in Canton, Ohio, early on New Year's Day 1953.

That dramatic death alone would have granted the Alabama-born singer legendary status in the annals of popular music. That he so eloquently documented his own troubled life in song, fought a hard losing battle with drinking and drugs, and still notched up seven #1 singles and sold over 11 million records makes him an icon, his work a standard by which all country artists are judged, even today.

Hank Williams was born Hiram King Williams on September 17, 1923, in the poor rural community of Mount Olive, Alabama. His music would focus on isolation and loneliness, a product of his solitary childhood. Spina bifida occulta, a debilitating spinal defect, limited his physical capabilities, and when the boy was just six years old his father was hospitalized for years with an aneurism. Hank saw him just a couple of times during his childhood. His mother moved the family from town to town, trying to make money running boarding houses in Depression-scarred Alabama.

Hank sang in church, joined the choir at six, and received a $3.50 Silvertone guitar as a gift from his mother when he was eight years old; he was taught the fundamentals on the instrument by a local bluesman, Rufus "Tee-Tot" Payne. Williams told Ralph Gleason in

April 1951, in a *San Francisco Chronicle* interview, "I learned to play guitar from an old colored man. He was named Tee-Tot, and he played in a colored street band. I was shinin' shoes, sellin' newspapers, and followin' [him] around to get him to teach me to play the guitar. I'd give him fifteen cents or whatever I could get hold of for a lesson. When I was about eight years old, I got my first guitar. It was a secondhand one that my mother bought for me for $3.50."

Hank had developed a liking for alcohol before he was a teenager, mostly while attending wild parties at the home of his cousins, the McNeills, in Monroe County. Saturday nights were all about tuning in to the *Grand Ole Opry* radio show. Inspired by the stars he heard there, Williams formed his own band, the Drifting Cowboys, played on a local Montgomery radio station, and picked up gigs in the area.

In 1944, he married Audrey Sheppard, a wannabe singer herself who played bass and sang with Hank's bands. But most significantly, she championed her gifted but wayward husband's music, playing a vital role in getting him to Nashville, where she set up a meeting with music publisher Fred Rose.

Rose, a business partner of *Grand Ole Opry* star Roy Acuff and a successful songwriter, was impressed by Williams and signed him to a recording deal with Sterling Records, but the talented newcomer quickly moved to the much bigger MGM label the following year. Although already virtually an alcoholic, he was booked as a regular on the *Opry*'s biggest radio rival,

the *Louisiana Hayride*, and made his chart debut with "Move It on Over" in 1947.

Williams hit the big time with "Lovesick Blues" in 1949, by which time he and the band were pulling in more than $1,000 a show, huge money in the 1940s. He scored a staggering seven hits in that one year, including "Wedding Bells," "Mind Your Own Business," "You're Gonna Change (or I'm Gonna Leave)," and "My Bucket's Got a Hole in It."

On June 11, 1949, Hank Williams made country music history with his *Grand Ole Opry* debut. After rocking his way through the upbeat "Lovesick Blues," he was brought back onstage by the screaming fans for a record-breaking six encores. Williams would play the *Opry* regularly over the next few years, as his hit-making became prolific.

In 1950, he scored hits with classic tunes like "Long Gone Lonesome Blues," "Why Don't You Love Me," "Moanin' the Blues," "I Just Don't Like This Kind of Livin'," "My Son Calls Another Man Daddy," "They'll Never Take Her Love from Me," "Why Should We Try," and "Nobody's Lonesome for Me." Not content with that slew of country masterpieces, Williams also released spiritual records under the name of Luke the Drifter.

Further hits, including "Hey, Good Lookin'," "Howlin' at the Moon," "Crazy Heart," "Lonesome Whistle," "Baby, We're Really in Love," "Honky-Tonk Blues," "Half as Much," "Jambalaya," "Settin' the Woods on Fire," "You Win Again," and "I'll Never Get Out of This World Alive," kept Williams almost permanently in the country music Top 10 throughout 1951 and 1952.

So popular were some of his songs that mainstream starts like Tony Bennett, Jo Stafford, Kay Starr, and Frankie Laine recorded versions, an unprecedented achievement for a country artist at a time when "hillbilly" music was given scant respect within the music industry as a whole.

But behind the music there was another story unfolding. The apparently confident performer onstage

Western swing pioneer Bob Wills, in his trademark Stetson in a 1940s publicity shot.

was frequently a shambling bag of nerves offstage. The articulate artist fans heard on the radio was too often in reality a slurring drunk, drinking whiskey and popping pills to ward off both fame-induced demons and the constant pain of his permanent back condition.

It all caught up with him in the last few months of 1952. His drinking had caused the *Grand Ole Opry* to fire him (hopefully as a warning), and his wife, Audrey, filed for divorce. He remarried and kept up a relentless workload, but by the end of 1952 he was breaking down, physically, mentally, and spiritually. He wouldn't live to see more than a couple of hours of 1953.

Despite his outlaw ways, drinking and drug use, unreliability, and sometimes unpleasant demeanor, Williams was respected by the music industry of the day—and was a hero to millions of fans across America.

TEXAS MUSIC

BELOW

An 1886 map of Hill County, Texas, in the south of which (directly north of McLennan County) can be found Willie's birthplace of Abbot.

With music playing such a significant role in his home life during Nelson's formative years, it's no wonder that he and his sister, Bobbie, would be entranced by the sounds coming from the family radio. Much of what they heard was the popular music of the day, from jazz to big band swing. But being in Texas, there was also the increasingly popular country and western music, as it was labeled at that time—with a heavy emphasis on the western, as far as cowboy movie fan Willie was concerned.

The history of country music in Texas reflects the cultural makeup of one of the most diverse communities in the United States, which also embraces blues, jazz, spirituals, gospel, rock-and-roll, Tex-Mex, Mexican, Cajun, and the music of Czechs, Germans, British, and other European immigrants.

The early pioneers, along with Latinos from across the Mexican border and Native Americans, were joined in the nineteenth century by immigrants from all over the world. In the 1820s, families from the Southern states were encouraged to travel west to Texas, taking with them their music. Significantly, they were often accompanied by their slaves, who of course had their own unique music. And by the late 1830s, the immigrant population included settlers from England, Ireland, Scotland, Germany, Czechoslovakia, Poland, and Italy. It was a melting pot in action. Immigrant life was tough, encouraging the various groups to integrate rather than developing distinctly separate communities.

Diversity of sound was key, as Nelson recalled during an interview for PBS's *Oral Histories*: "Well, I heard everything. We lived just across the street from two houses of Mexicans, they played their music day and night with their radio. So I was educated early in life on 'south of the border' music. Most of the people that I lived and grew up with around there in Abbot

Vernon Dalhart

ABOVE

Born in 1883, Vernon Dalhart
was literally a singing cowboy,
having herded cattle as a
teenager before his career
as a vocalist took off, during
which he made over five
thousand records under
a variety of pseudonyms
through the 1920s and '30s.

were Czechoslovakians. I learned a lot of polkas and
waltzes. And from working in the fields with a lot
of the black folks there, I learned a lot of blues. And
working and going to church, I learned gospel. So I was
pretty educated on a lot of different kinds of music while I was still pretty young."

Country music in Texas evolved in its own distinctive way, with the cowboy or
western element being predominant. The roots of cowboy culture can be traced
back to the great cattle drives of the nineteenth century, when Mexican vaqueros
and American cowboys (a quarter of whom were liberated slaves) drove herds
from Texas to the Midwest along famous routes such as the Chisholm Trail and
the Goodnight-Loving Trail. Out of this came the mythology of the Wild West,
first via cheap dime novels and then by the cowboy songs and ballads that became
hugely popular with the advent of phonograph records.

In 1924, a classically trained Texan singer, (and part-time cowboy) Vernon
Dalhart recorded "The Wreck of the Old 97," which sold a staggering million

copies. Suddenly cowboy songs were big business, a popularity boosted with the arrival of sound movies in the late 1920s. Through the '30s and '40s, Hollywood made huge stars of "singing cowboys" (John Wayne was one of the earliest), including Gene Autry, Tex Ritter, and Roy Rogers.

But the biggest driving force in the evolution of country music was the spread of radio station networks across the United States during the 1920s, and the simultaneous development of the recording industry. During the minor recession of the early 1920s (which was mild compared to the extreme economic fallout of the '30s), country music offered singers and musicians a way out of poverty with a decent living to be made playing on radio stations and making records. Many aimed for the kind of million-selling success that country's first real superstar, Jimmie Rodgers, enjoyed in the 1920s. And as a result of this boom, there followed a major cross-fertilization of styles and genres. As Nashville became the industry mecca for country music, thanks to a proliferation of music publishing companies, so the *Grand Ole Opry* radio show on WSM in Nashville established itself as the gold standard of country music broadcasting.

"I REMEMBER WHEN WE USED TO SIT AROUND AND WATCH THE RADIO, BECAUSE IT WAS NEW IN THE HOUSE. THERE WAS SOMETHIN' THERE THAT HAD SOME ENTERTAINMENT COMIN' OUT OF IT."

—WILLIE NELSON

"I remember when we used to sit around and watch the radio," Nelson told Bud Young of *Goldmine* magazine in January 1995, "because it was new in the house. There was somethin' there that had some entertainment comin' out of it. The first thing that we tuned in was WSM in Nashville, the *Grand Ole Opry.* That was a regular. And everything else. I turned the dial."

Such was the power of the WSM transmitter in Nashville that the show could be listened to by music fans all over the South. The show launched an athlete-turned-singer by the name of Roy Acuff to national acclaim and unimagined fame, wealth, and political influence. Acuff became the featured star on the *Grand Ole*

Opry, and by 1943 was earning himself a cool $200,000 a year. He played a strain of Appalachian mountain music, or hillbilly as it was known at the time. But while religious lyrics and music based on European folk songs worked well in the conservative southeast, in the rural wild west of Texas people preferred dance music as an escape from the everyday worries of life during the Depression. So one style that emerged in Texas, and in neighboring Oklahoma, was western swing, an amalgam of big band swing music, Dixieland jazz, blues, and the western sound

BELOW

Roy Acuff, with Kitty Wells, the "Queen of Country Music," ca. 1955. Wells toured with Acuff and his band, the Smoky Mountain Boys, and they often shared the bill on the *Grand Ole Opry* in the 1940s.

of polkas and cowboy tunes. The bands showcased some outstanding musicians, many of them jazz players tempted to the new style for both musical enrichment and better pay. Bob Wills, while not the inventor of the genre, became its most beloved exponent in the 1940s. His Texas Playboys featured a dance-centric lineup of acoustic guitar, fiddle, saxophones, and electric and pedal steel guitar, soaring through the lead melodies.

A contemporary of western swing was honky-tonk, which shot through the airwaves and dance floors in the 1940s via new acts such as Ernest Tubb, Ray Price, and Hank Williams. Tubb was the early leader of this hard-edged, prototype rock-and-roll that blasted out of Texas and Oklahoma honky-tonk dance halls; his 1943 hit "Walkin' the Floor over You" was the first song young Willie Nelson learned to play from listening to the radio.

OPPOSITE

Willie Nelson on acoustic guitar in 1955 (second from the left), as a member of the Texans, the band formed by his sister, Bobbie (second right), and brother-in-law, Bud Fletcher.

MUSIC TAKES OVER

Willie and his older sister, Bobbie, were raised simply and humbly in Abbott. The first home they lived in was on the outskirts of town, a typical country dwelling with vegetable patch, hogs, cows, and a well for water. His grandfather was a blacksmith, and young Willie spent a lot of time at the blacksmith's shop, watching and learning how to shoe horses.

Willie's grandfather died from a pneumonia attack when the boy was just seven years old. Losing an income was a hardship for the family, and they moved to another home, this time on the northern side of Abbott.

Grandmother Nancy continued to hold the family together as best she could, working as a cook and teacher at the local school. Bobbie and Willie supplemented the family income when they could, doing farm work and picking cotton, as did most of the local farmers' kids in the area. It was backbreaking work for little financial compensation, and a major factor in Willie's move toward music as a career.

The eleven-year-old Nelson had been making up his own songs for two or three years when he put together his first handmade song book, *Songs by Willie Nelson*, placing it on the family coffee table next to songbooks by stars of the day, including Jimmie Rodgers and Bing Crosby.

When she was just sixteen, Bobbie married a fiddle player named Bud Fletcher. Some time before their wedding, pianist Bobbie and Bud put together a dance band, the Texans, and included Willie on acoustic guitar. The band played dances all over their local area and even won a regular Sunday morning spot on a radio station, KHBR, in the neighboring town of Hillsboro.

Although music and the church may have been the bedrock of his upbringing, Willie also enjoyed the regular adolescent pursuits of sports, part-time jobs, smoking, drinking, and girls. He soon came to the conclusion that absolutes didn't really exist: churchgoers were not absolutely good, and barhoppers, smokers, and those perhaps outside the law were not absolutely bad—an approach he would adopt throughout his career.

Willie told Chet Flippo in the July 13, 1978, issue of *Rolling Stone*, "I think there's a big freedom in Texas that gives a person a right to move around and think and do what he wants to do. And I was taught this way: anybody from Texas could do whatever they fucking wanted to do. And that confidence, shit, if you got that going for you, you can do almost anything. I believe that has a lot to do with it."

Bob Wills

"Bob Wills was my hero in those days," Willie Nelson told PBS. "He was a bandleader. He had an incredible association and relation with his band. They watched him all the time, and he only had to nod or point his fiddle bow, and they would play. And they respected him a lot, and it was mutual respect. So I always thought that he was the greatest bandleader that I had seen."

Bob Wills was far more than a musician. He was a songwriter, a recording artist who sold over twenty million records, and he also appeared in over twenty-five movies. More than that, he was a charismatic cigar-chomping showman, famed for his onstage cry to his steel guitar player, "Take it away, Leon."

By the 1940s he was the top bandleader in the USA, earning himself a cool $350,000 a year. Wills may not have invented the jazz-infused country music labeled western swing, but nobody made that melodic dance sound more popular in pre-rock-and-roll America than Bob Wills and his Texas Playboys.

Wills was born as James Robert (Jim Rob) on March 6, 1905, just outside Kosse, a small town in Limestone County, Texas. Wills remains Kosse's most notable claim to fame, just ahead of the Wild West outlaw John Wesley Hardin, who shot a pimp dead there back in 1872. He grew up surrounded by nine brothers and sisters. His father was a cotton farmer and a state fiddle champion, who naturally had the Wills kids learn instruments and play at local dances at weekends. Later the Wills the family moved to Turkey, Texas.

Bob Wills became a barber, but continued playing fiddle when he could. In 1923, he married Edna Posey and moved to New Mexico, still finding employment cutting hair. Six years later, when the couple had a child, Bob decided it was time to make music his full-time occupation. His first regular gig was doing "blackface" comedy, part of a minstrel band that traveled the state in a medicine show—a touring variety show that peddled "miracle cure" patent medicines between the various acts.

That experience gave him the money and confidence to go out as a bandleader, and he formed the Wills Fiddle Band. The outfit was moderately successful, but did much better after a year or so when vocalist Milton Brown joined and the band was renamed the Light Crust Doughboys. Good enough for a record company to show interest, the band recorded for Victor in 1932.

Milton Brown was later replaced by Tommy Duncan, but by this time Wills had developed a heavy drinking habit that eventually got him kicked out of the Doughboys in 1933. Wills took Duncan with him, and along with his banjo-playing brother Johnnie Lee, they formed a new outfit, Bob Wills and the Texas Playboys. Initially the band played small-town dances, and as many radio shows as they could fit in. Wills understood his audiences, giving them a fun-fueled mix of jazz, country, swing, and blues within a heavily dance-oriented format. As the band became more popular he was able to increase its size, and by the early 1940s it

had eighteen members, drawing huge crowds around the country.

In 1940, Wills had a huge national hit with his recording of "San Antonio Rose," which made him a big star across America. Hollywood beckoned, and numerous movie appearances included *Take Me Back to Oklahoma* and *Go West Young Lady*. By the late 1940s, the Texas Playboys were outselling America's top swing bands, outfits fronted by household names like Tommy Dorsey and Benny Goodman.

But the swing era was drawing to a close, and through the 1950s even the popular Bob Wills was

Hank Williams at the height of his fame as country music's greatest superstar, broadcasting on the WSM radio station—home of the *Grand Ole Opry*.

forced to cut back on musicians and focus more on fiddle and steel guitar. Still a hero in Texas and Oklahoma, he toured almost constantly until a heart attack in the mid 1960s forced him to reduce his workload. But Bob Wills continued to record until suffering a stroke in December 1973, and finally passing away in the spring of 1975.

Nelson was popular at Abbott High School, where he was a decent halfback on the school football team, a guard on the basketball team, and shortstop on the baseball team. And he wasn't afraid to work for extra money, even if the pay wasn't as much as he'd pick up from playing music. One part-time job he made the most of was helping his sister as a phone operator. As he told *Texas Monthly* in December 2005, "Whenever the operators would take a vacation, they would hire her to run the board, and I would come in and help her. All the time I was sitting there, I'd be listening in to the conversations going on all over Abbott. I tapped every phone in town! I knew everything about the whole county."

High school finished for Nelson in 1950, followed by an uncomfortable stint in the U.S. Air Force, which fortunately ended after nine months when a back problem brought him early discharge. It could be said his anti-authoritarian temperament was diametrically opposed to the military ethos, and from the start of his short service, Willie was at odds with all the rules and regulations—not to mention being woken up at the crack of dawn every morning.

After his brief career in the air force, Willie attended Baylor University in Waco, Texas (he still jokes that he majored in dominoes), where he studied agriculture, but all the time music was becoming his main preoccupation. After dropping out of college, he subsidized casual gigging work with a variety of jobs, including tree trimmer, saddle maker, auto parts worker, and nightclub bouncer

FIRST LOVE

It was following a low-key gig in Waco that Willie first spied a young dark-haired waitress serving hamburgers in a drive-thru burger joint. He was instantly smitten, and although he was knocked back several times, the two teens eventually began dating. Despite the bad example of his own parents' marriage, the couple were married by a justice of the peace just three months later. Martha Matthews was just sixteen, and Willie still only eighteen. Initially they lived with Mama Nelson, relying on Willie's sporadic music jobs and part-time work, while Martha continued to work as a waitress. Becoming well known around the Abbott music scene, Willie finally won himself an audition to be a disk jockey on a nearby radio station in Pleasanton, Texas.

He told *Country Song Roundup* in February 1969 that "My test was to do fifteen minutes of news . . . live . . . the first time I'd ever been on the air as an announcer.

"I WAS TAUGHT THIS WAY: ANYBODY FROM TEXAS COULD DO WHATEVER THEY . . . WANTED TO DO. AND THAT CONFIDENCE, IF YOU GOT THAT GOING FOR YOU, YOU CAN DO ALMOST ANYTHING." —WILLIE NELSON

Then he gave me a commercial to do. It was for the Pleasanton Pharmacy. It went like this . . . 'The Pleasanton Pharmacy Pharmaceutical department accurately and precisely fills your doctor's prescription,' and after I got through with that, he knew I'd never done radio work. It was the hardest commercial I've ever done. He gave me the job anyway. Then he worked with me to show me all about radio work."

Less than a year after their wedding, Martha and Willie became parents themselves, as they welcomed Lana Nelson into the world. The responsibility of being a parent encouraged the still-teenage Willie to find more and better paid work to support his new family. But the pressure of raising a child also served to intensify the already tempestuous nature of the couple's marital relationship. It was passionate, in both good and bad ways, and after one particularly unpleasant marital altercation, Willie suggested a change of scenery might be good for all of them.

Who, Him?

Why, he's yer cotton-pickin', snuff-dippin', tobacca-chewin', stump-jumpin', gravy-soppin', coffee-pot-dodgin', dumplin-eatin', frog-giggin', hillbilly from Hill County, Texas . . .

WILLIE NELSON!

Just rode into town to take over his own show on KVAN . . . an' this young fella fits right in, here at the station with the sense of humor. See that pan-handled description up there? Them's his very own words! Willie's got wit, warmth and wow . . . and once you hear "Western Express" you'll agree!

He's no newcomer to radio though. Been entertaining folks since he was sweet 15 . . . and for the past 3 ½ years, he's been a big name in Ft. Worth on station KCNC. But now he's moved "kit 'n kaboodle" to Portland. An' ya know what? He likes rain!

You'll like **him** . . . an' you'll get your "enjoys" listening to Texas Willie Nelson on "Western Express", 2:30 to 3:30 Monday through Saturday on KVAN.

 **on your dial**

"the station with the sense of humor"

Just as his mother, Myrtle, had done some twenty years before, Nelson opted to head out west. He saw an advertisement in the local newspaper for drivers to take cars across the country. All he needed was to find $50 and he could drive his family all the way to California. It was a tremendous deal, except for the fact that Willie only had $25 to his name. Being a popular character from a well-respected family, he was able to borrow the rest of the money needed, sign on the dotted line, and get Martha and Lana to San Diego without too much trouble.

Unfortunately, once they reached California, opportunities were not as ample as they had hoped, and only Martha was able to find work in San Diego. Undeterred, Willie chose to hitchhike roughly one thousand miles to Portland, Oregon, where his mother lived.

There he planned to stay with Myrtle, find some well-paid work, and send for his wife and daughter when things were looking secure. Given the fractious nature of Willie and Myrtle's relationship since the abandonment of Willie as a baby, the mother and son reunion was remarkably successful. But while Nelson could certainly find work, the positions he truly wanted in the music business were few and far between. Then, just as he was beginning to despair of ever achieving the kind of stability he needed to bring the family together, he secured an on-air presenter position at a radio station just across the river from Portland in Vancouver, Washington.

RADIO DAYS

Through 1956, his *Western Express* daily KVAN radio show saw the Texas singer-songwriter introduce himself on every show as a "cotton-pickin', snuff-dippin', tobacca-chewin', stump-jumpin', gravy-soppin', coffee-pot-dodgin', dumplin-eatin', frog-giggin', hillbilly from Hill County, Texas." The colorful intro, as well as his skill for picking records and talking over them, earned Willie Nelson a modest $40 a week; it also gave him the media exposure that enabled him to promote gigs, perform in local clubs, make records, and write songs. He was soon doing well enough to buy his family a home, and he took advantage of the radio station's equipment to record his first single, "No Place for Me." The record sold three thousand copies, a modest start for Willie, who now had a music-centered living going for him in Vancouver.

But Willie was spending more and more time writing songs, and felt he was becoming good at it. By chance, Mae Axton, the writer of Elvis Presley's first big hit, "Heartbreak Hotel," was a guest at the radio station while she was working with Elvis's manager Tom Parker and country star Hank Snow. Nelson took the opportunity to pick her brains about songwriting, and Axton immediately warmed to the shy and unassuming twenty-three-year-old who was nevertheless determined to speak to her.

After hearing Willie's latest tune, "Family Bible," Axton was deeply touched by the authenticity of the lyrics, and urged him to leave the Pacific Northwest and get back to the heartland of country music. She advised him to move back to Texas, where there was a vibrant country music scene that could sustain a good living for a performer—or even better, he should try his luck in Nashville, since he clearly had the talent to write songs at a professional level.

Enthused and inspired by Mae Axton's encouragement, when he was denied a pay rise by KVAN shortly afterward, Willie took her advice and moved back to Texas. But he also had in mind, as a final destination, Music City USA—Nashville—which was by now the headquarters of the thriving country music industry.

OPPOSITE

Publicity material for "Texas" Willie Nelson's *Western Express* show, broadcast on KVAN out of Vancouver, Washington.

Willie, his pregnant wife, and their two kids (their second daughter, Susie, was born in Vancouver, Washington, in January 1957) aimed the car at Texas, but on the way stopped in Denver, Colorado, where the owner of a club called Hart's Corner booked him as a house band guitar player for a few weeks.

From Denver it was on to Springfield, Missouri, where the Nelsons stayed with country singer Billy Walker, who Martha and Willie knew from the Texas 'tonk circuit. By this time Walker was a performer on the *Ozark Jubilee* country TV show, and as a favor, he arranged for Willie to get an audition with the show's producer, Si Simon. Nelson failed to impress on this occasion, and instead took the only job available, dishwasher at Aunt Martha's Pancake House. Martha found employment waitressing again, and Nelson stuck it out until he couldn't clean another plate, glass, or cup.

SALESMAN

Then the Nelson gang headed south again, this time aiming for Waco, Texas, and then on to Fort Worth, where Willie's birth father, Ira, was living. The family stayed with Ira in Fort Worth, and, determined to be a provider and good father to his kids, Nelson all but retired from the music game and transformed himself into a door-to-door salesman. Suited and booted, his hair neatly combed, Willie Nelson left the cowboy image behind for his new career.

"You name it, I sold it," he told the UK's *Daily Telegraph* in 2013. "I sold encyclopedias door to door, bibles, vacuum cleaners. I wanted to make a living for my family while I was trying to get by in the music business and if you were gonna be a salesman you had to dress the part."

To supplement the salesman income, Nelson also taught kids' Sunday school at the Metropolitan Baptist Church. At night Nelson continued to pick up his guitar and play in the numerous clubs and bars around Fort Worth. When the pastor of the Baptist church realized that his Sunday school teacher was singing in bars that seethed with gyrating bodies, loud music, and alcohol, Nelson was fired. Given that many of the bar patrons were church regulars, the hypocrisy shown by the pastor affected the Methodist-raised Nelson to such an extent that he began reading about alternative religions, developing his personalized religious philosophy, as he explained to Chet Flippo of *Rolling Stone* magazine in 1978: "I am religious, even though I don't go to church. I believe in reincarnation. We're taught to believe that all men are created equal and yet we know that one guy is born without eyes and one guy is born *with* eyes. So that's not equal. They had to be born together in the beginning. At one time, we were all born at the same time. God imagines everyone, so we're all images of him—in the *beginning*. He made us all in the beginning and since then we've been coming back and forth. First time we came in we knew a lot and we've lost it along the way. Being down here is kinda like goin' through the university: you go through one grade at a time and if you fail, you gotta go back and take those tests again."

Despite the birth of his first son, Willie Hugh Nelson Jr., on May 21, 1958, Nelson had become very aware, once again, that a conformist life really wasn't for him. He wrote more songs and decided to try his musical luck in a bigger city, this time Houston.

"WE'RE TAUGHT TO BELIEVE THAT ALL MEN ARE CREATED EQUAL AND YET WE KNOW THAT ONE GUY IS BORN WITHOUT EYES AND ONE GUY IS BORN WITH EYES. SO THAT'S NOT EQUAL." —WILLIE NELSON

After small-town communities like Waco and Fort Worth, oil-town Houston seemed a vast and sprawling city to Nelson. Everywhere was miles from everywhere. The city was impersonal and it was difficult for a new family locating there to adjust to it. He found an apartment in a Houston suburb, Pasadena, and focused on finding paid work in the wild and raucous nightclubs, bars, and honky-tonks along the Gulf Freeway. The hours he spent driving his car, hustling for work, allowed Nelson plenty of time to think and, crucially, to write songs. In a few weeks of running around Houston absorbing the city's highs and lows, he had written "Night Life," "Crazy," and "Mr. Record Man," songs that would help put him on the musical map in the very near future.

PAUL BUSKIRK

Reconnecting with various old faces from the Texas country and bar scene, Nelson played some of his best songs to another musician, Paul Buskirk. Buskirk was a mandolin and guitar luminary who'd played over the years with top names like Lefty Frizzell, the Louvin Brothers, and Chet Atkins. He also ran a guitar school in Houston, and he gave Nelson a job teaching. The only problem was that Nelson was self-taught and played by ear. So, in order to teach the kids the correct way to play, Buskirk would teach Nelson a lesson one week, who would then pass it on before getting another lesson from Buskirk the next week.

The scheme worked out, as Nelson told Austin Scaggs of *Rolling Stone* in 2004: "I was taught by Paul Buskirk, and his approach was using the Mel Bay books. Guitar lessons like *Teaching Little Fingers to Play*—where you'd start out in Lesson One and go all the way through Seven. But I stayed a couple lessons ahead of my pupils [laughs], and now and then I'd play a hot lick of the blues just to impress them a little bit."

Buskirk also agreed to inject a little cash into Nelson's wallet by getting a couple of pals to go in with him and buy Willie's songs "Family Bible" and "Night Life." They gave him $200 for both tunes, and in 1960 Buskirk went into the studio with Claude Gray and recorded "Family Bible," managing to get it released on D Records. D Records was a relatively new label started by Starday Records founder Pappy Daily, who had enjoyed tremendous success out of Houston with the signing of local talent and with country music legend George Jones through the 1950s.

"Family Bible" was Claude Gray's second record release. He was working as a disc jockey for radio station

WDAL out of Meridian, Mississippi, when his 1959 debut "I'm Not Supposed" made the country charts in *Cashbox* magazine. By the time the Willie Nelson tune was released, he had already made appearances on such nationally known shows as *Louisiana Hayride* on KWKH in Shreveport, Louisiana, and *The Big "D" Jamboree* over KRLD out of Dallas–Fort Worth.

Buskirk, already a champion of Nelson's skills, got Willie a recording contract with D Records. Willie cut his very first single, "A Man with the Blues." But when it was released, the record made no headway whatsoever. Next, Buskirk got Nelson into the nearby Gold Star studios in Houston and recorded "Misery Mansion" and "What a Way to Live." It was released as a single, but again, neither side managed to garner any attention.

Nelson also recorded a version of "Night Life." Steel guitar luminary Herb Remington played on the track. He remembered that label owner Pappy Daily just hated Nelson's efforts, telling the *Houston Press* in 2013, "Pappy had a good ear but he just wanted hits, and to him most hits sounded pretty much the same. He hated 'Night Life' partly because he despised what he called 'musician's music.' Nothing drove Pappy crazier than a bunch of us jamming. He didn't like it or get it. And he sure didn't want to pay for it." "Nightlife" was subsequently released on Rx Records as "Paul Buskirk and the Little Men featuring Hugh Nelson."

LARRY BUTLER

With his recent experience selling Bibles and books door to door, Nelson applied the same tactics to finding some gigs. He would drop by clubs and bars that presented live music, and sniff out any opportunities for playing, either solo or as part of a band. At Houston's famed Esquire Ballroom one afternoon, Nelson waited patiently until Larry Butler and his band had finished daily rehearsals before asking the bandleader if he could use another guitar player or singer. Butler said no, explaining the situation to Nelson. Used to thinking on his feet as a salesman, Willie quickly offered instead to sell him songs for just ten dollars each. Nelson played several for him, including "Mr. Record Man," "Crazy," "Nightlife," and "What a Way to Live." At this point the financially strapped Nelson could have been scalped by Larry Butler, like many songwriters before and since have been taken advantage of by dishonest musicians. He was desperate, vulnerable, and ripe for picking. But fortune smiled, and Butler, a decent man, recognized Nelson's genuine writing talent and refused to buy them for just a few dollars. But he did come up with something.

Larry Butler, remembers the day well. Speaking to the *Houston Press* he said, "I told him I wasn't going to buy them; they were too good to just give away like that." Instead, sympathetic to Nelson's financial embarrassment, Larry Butler loaned Willie $50, which he could pay off by playing in the band. Butler was so impressed by Nelson that when the owner of the Esquire Ballroom refused to pay

OPPOSITE

An eager-looking Willie

Nelson in the early 1960s,

just as the budding

songwriter was hitting

Nashville for the first time.

for another musician, Butler chose to divide up his own $25 a night in order to pay to Nelson a minimal wage for his guitar and vocal chores.

The magnanimous Butler even encouraged Nelson to sing a few songs with the band in the evenings. To supplement that money, Nelson found a low-paying day job as a DJ at Pasadena country music radio station KRCT (650 AM), drawing on his previous radio experience.

The nightlife pretty much put a stop to the day job, however, because Nelson simply couldn't keep the candle burning at both ends. Station owner Leroy Golger fired him, a decision that only motivated Nelson to finally give Nashville a chance, especially since Claude Gray's version of "Family Bible" went Top 10 in the *Billboard* country singles chart in early 1960. Nelson had already sold his royalty rights to the song, so there was no more money to be enjoyed, but it did at least give him confidence that songwriting was indeed the path he needed to follow. Houston just wasn't working in terms of getting to the next level, and with a speeding arrest in August of that year, Nelson figured it was time to make that move to Nashville. It seemed like a now-or-never moment, so he dropped Martha and the kids with her family in Waco and headed east to Tennessee in a beat-up old 1946 Buick.

NASHVILLE

Nashville was a town that WSM presenter David Cobb had memorably dubbed as "Music City USA" in 1950, a city where a promising music business cottage industry was on the verge of spectacular change. The story of Nashville's rise to prominence in the music business starts in the 1920s with the success of WSM, a vastly influential and powerful 50,000-watt AM radio station. The station worked as a promotional vehicle for a local insurance company, National Life and Accident Insurance Company, who used the slogan "We Shield Millions," or WSM.

Executives of the insurance company felt that WSM radio and its early programs and personalities would help their sales agents have an easier time selling insurance when they knocked on doors in the rural South. Ads for the company mentioned their ownership of WSM. The day after Christmas 1925, WSM went on the air with a weekly Saturday night program. It was hosted by George D. Hay, and during the 1930s that one-hour show quickly developed into the station's flagship program—*The Grand Ole Opry*—a barnstorming four-hour. Free tickets were offered to listeners to watch the show live, and after outgrowing four venues in Nashville, the *Opry* made its home in the Ryman Auditorium, a red-brick former church on Fifth Avenue, just off bustling Broadway. The auditorium was a little shabby and had no air-conditioning, and fans sat on old church pews— but the acoustics were magnificent. Artists and fans came from all over the southern United States to attend *Grand Ole Opry* performances.

726

EARL BARTON MUSIC inc.

BILL ANDERSON *enterprises*

MARPAT MUSIC PUBLISHERS, inc.

KA$H RECORDS

₡entral ♪ongs, ℐnc.

mar *Records* Lenox Music

Par-Co. Enterprises Corp.

gold Standard RECORDS
A Zeke Clements Enterprise

Mar-Co. Artist Corp.

In the 1940s, WSM made the smart move of opening up their audio equipment to musicians, allowing them to record locally rather than trekking to Chicago or New York City. The country crooner Eddy Arnold made what's widely regarded as the first contemporary country recording, "Mommy Please Stay Home with Me," at the WSM studio in December 1944. The engineers on the sessions saw the potential in recording artists in Nashville and set up studios in the old Tulane Hotel. These were the city's top studios in the 1940s and 1950s, until another WSM employee, bandleader Owen Bradley, with his brother Harold, built the Quonset Hut studio in 1958. It was situated away from downtown Nashville, around 16th and 17th Avenues South. Other record companies moved into the area, including the famed RCA Studio B, where Elvis recorded many hits with producer Chet Atkins. In a short time, a slew of small studios and record company offices opened up in the wooden A-frame houses on the west side of Nashville. Soon the district around 16th, 17th, and 18th Avenues would become known around the world as Music Row.

THE STORE

Willie Nelson often refers to Nashville at that time as "the store." He understood that the city, despite the artistic community that lived there, was essentially a hub for companies that bought and sold songs. On his arrival in town, he drove directly to Music Row, where his old gray Buick finally gave up the ghost. He was, however, in Nashville—a town that would bring mixed blessings, including plenty of highs and some very low lows.

Things looked bad for Nelson when he first arrived; he had to spend his first night in a seedy establishment that was more hostel and shelter than hotel. He had enough cash for breakfast in a local coffee shop that first morning in town, which is where he had his first slice of good luck in the new city. In walked Billy Walker, an old friend from Texas and the man who had previously given the Nelson family a place to stay in Missouri. Walker had left the *Ozark Jubilee* show and was now working on the *Grand Ole Opry*, as he endeavored to build his own country music career.

Walker, naturally, offered Nelson a place to stay and drove the carless Willie to the Music Row offices of numerous publishing companies, where Nelson played his best songs for the executives and song pluggers. Unfortunately, at that point nobody was interested in his unusual singing and writing style, and Willie fell back on selling encyclopedias, courtesy of another Billy Walker contact in Nashville.

It wasn't what Nelson wanted, but he was a decent salesman and the commissions allowed him to send for Martha and the kids. The family set up shop in a $25-a-week trailer in the less-than-wholesome Dunn's Trailer Court. (Country songwriter and singer Roger Miller stayed there before Nelson and used the park's "Trailers for Sale or Rent" sign for the inspiration of his classic 1965 song "King of the Road.")

Martha's superior waitressing skills secured her a job at the Hitching Post honky-tonk in downtown Nashville almost immediately, and the family had enough to live, but little more. It took time for Nelson to figure out the rhythms, rhymes, and particular ways of Music City. Knocking on publishing company doors was clearly not the way to go, so he began hanging out in the evening with some kindred spirit songwriters at one particular downtown bar, Tootsie's Orchid Lounge.

TOOTSIE'S

Now probably the most famous honky-tonk in the world, back in 1960 Tootsie's, like Willie Nelson, was fairly new on the scene. Both would play a significant role in the new wave of country music that writers like Willie, Kris Kristofferson, Hank Cochran, Roger Miller, Harlan Howard, Merle Kilgore, Mel Tillis, and other Tootsie's regulars were about to unleash on the previously conservative sounds of contemporary country music. Top songwriter Harlan Howard told me in 1988, "Nashville's a small town now, but back in the '60s it was really a close-knit community, and we writers looked out for each other, supported each other. It was a real community spirit we had."

Before Tootsie's became Tootsie's, it was called Mom's. In 1960, Hattie Louise "Tootsie" Bess bought the establishment, recognizing the value of its location next to the home of the *Grand Ole Opry*, Ryman Auditorium, and renamed it Tootsie's Orchid Lounge. Named for the new paint job Bess had done when she moved into the bar, the outside of the building certainly stands out from its more nondescript neighbors—but it's the back of Tootsie's that really put the establishment on the Nashville map.

The Ryman, being an old church, was dry, with no alcohol allowed under any circumstance. So many of the *Grand Ole Opry* performers took advantage of the bar's proximity to the stage on a Saturday night. The artists would listen to the live *Opry* radio broadcast in the bar, so as to know when to get back to the Ryman in time for their cue to go onstage.

Tootsies had no liquor license at that point— it was beer only—but even so the booze flowed freely. As Willie would so aptly say, "It's seventeen steps to Tootsie's—and thirty-four steps back." If the revelers were slow to leave come closing time, Tootsie herself would prod them on their way with a hatpin!

Grand Ole Opry legend Little Jimmy Dickens told *The Boot* in 2015: "If you missed a friend backstage, you knew where to go look for them. Because they would be in Tootsie's visiting with one another, trading songs around, or having a beer and visiting with one another, and I think that's one of the greatest things that ever happened to country music, because these songwriters all got together and wrote these beautiful songs that we hear today. As far as getting stuck with the hatpin by Tootsie, I was lucky, I never did get out of line, 'cause I learned early, you don't do that!"

But aside from *Opry* performers partaking of alcohol on weekends, Tootsie's in the early 1960s was home away from home for a new breed of songwriters and the obvious destination for those new to town who wanted to john the ranks of

Nashville's top tunesmiths. Country singer Bobby Bare told the *Nashville Scene* newspaper in 2010 that in the 1960s, "If they had dropped a bomb on Tootsie's at that time, the music industry would've gone hungry for songs for a while."

Tootsie's was the natural home for the new writers in the country music genre, many of them financially strapped. The ebullient and always kindhearted Tootsie would give her writers meals and drinks when they had no way to pay, and she'd even give them a place to stay from time to time. "Tootsie's was always a kind of magic place," Willie Nelson told the *Tennessean*. "Tootsie kept us going. She probably ran a bar tab for every down-and-out songwriter in town."

Initially Nelson, so used to writing and selling, tried to pitch his songs to these other writers before realizing that he was part of a new wave in Nashville. He had stumbled upon a hip, cutting-edge music community that would revolutionize country music in the next decade or so.

He told Phoenix.com in January 2002: "It was a time with Harlan Howard, Hank Cochran, Roger Miller.... It was the kind of Tin Pan Alley thing where everybody got together every morning, and we'd play the songs we'd written the night before. Or we'd go to somebody's house at night and pass the guitar around. There's not that kind of camaraderie going on these days in my life. I miss it a lot. There were a lot of great writers all around me."

But the transition from new kid in town to successful songwriter wasn't easy, nor was it quick. Nelson hated returning home to the family trailer and letting Martha know he'd been unsuccessful with his music. Their marriage, already rocky, became all the more volatile. Sometimes Martha would leave home for a few days after a nasty fight; other times Nelson would run off—mostly to Tootsie's, where he could always finds a meal, a bed, and, increasingly, alcohol.

One snowy winter night, a drunk and depressed Nelson decided to lie down for a rest on the street outside Tootsie's on Lower Broadway. He still doesn't know why, but he survived, and the incident seems to have brought a measure of calm to his search for success.

HOWARD AND COCHRAN

A week later, back at Tootsie's, another songwriter, Hank Cochran, told Nelson he truly believed that he had what it took to be a professional songwriter in Nashville. Cochran was a successful songwriter at that point. He had started out in the early '50s in a duo with future rock-and-roll idol Eddie Cochran (who was no relation), working as the Cochran Brothers. The pair played regularly on the West Coast, with Hank doing most of the vocals and Eddie handling lead guitar. Club dates led to a regular spot on the *California Hayride* television show and a recording contract for the Ekko label. The duo released a single, "Two Blue Singin' Stars," and "Mr. Fiddle." Although stardom didn't quite find the Cochran Brothers, they

ABOVE

Harlan Howard in his
makeshift Nashville recording
studio in the mid-1960s,
working with his second wife,
singer Jan Howard.

did get to tour with a big name of the time, Lefty Frizzell, and made useful music
business connections.

But with Eddie moving to rock-and-roll, the duo called it quits. In California,
Hank Cochran met another young songwriter, Harlan Howard. They both moved
to Nashville in 1960, and as the songwriting team of Howard and Cochran they
came up with the song "I Fall to Pieces." Patsy Cline took it to the top of the
charts in 1961. It was Cline's first #1 country record, topping the country chart
on August 7, 1961, and spending two weeks in the pole position. It was also a
Top 15 pop hit and reached the Top Ten on the Adult Contemporary chart.

Cochran had a contract with a Nashville publishing company, Pamper Music,
co-owned by James "Hal" Smith and the country music star Ray Price. Convinced
of Willie Nelson's talents, he arranged a meeting with Smith. He recalled the day
to Larry Wayne Clark for the International Songwriters' Association blog in 2002:
"'Well, I'll go in there and talk to Hal. What would you have to have?' He [Willie]
said, 'Well, I'd have to have $50 a week to at least live on till I get something
going.' And I said, 'Well, let me go in and talk to him.'"

Patsy Cline

Rolling Stone magazine voted Patsy Cline's version of Willie Nelson's song "Crazy" #85 of the Top 500 songs of all time. Recorded in 1961, it quickly became a pop crossover hit and is now a country music standard, sung in honky-tonks across the United States seven nights a week, every week of the year.

Cline, from Virginia, burst onto the country music scene in 1957, when she won the *Arthur Godfrey's Talent Scouts* television show with an emotional rendition of "Walkin' after Midnight." This put her on the charts and allowed her to become a member of the *Grand Old Opry*. In 1961, she had a country hit as well as a pop hit with the majestic "I Fall to Pieces."

The follow-up song, albeit much delayed, would be penned by Willie Nelson. But "Crazy" was by no means an obvious hit. Thanks to Hank Cochran getting him a publishing deal with Pamper Music, Nelson had recorded the song as a demo. Part spoken, the phrasing was off the beat, and there was little in the rambling performance to suggest a soon-to-be pop standard. Short on cash, as ever, Nelson hustled his songs to anyone who would listen, usually at the music biz watering hole Tootsie's Orchid Lounge.

"We were at Tootsie's Orchid in Nashville, and I had brought that song with me from Texas," Nelson recalled to Katie Cook for CMT *Hot 20 Countdown* in April 2015. "I had talked Tootsie into letting me put it on the jukebox and Charlie Dick, Patsy Cline's husband, was there. We were having a beer, listening to the song, and

he says, 'Patsy has to do this song.' I said, 'Well, maybe one day,' and he said, 'No. Now. Let's go play it for her.'

"So it was after midnight by then, and we woke Patsy up—he did—and I wouldn't get out of the car. But she came out and made me get out of the car. I went in and sang her the song, and she recorded the song the next week."

When it came time to record the song, Cline was nervous. A lot was resting on her next single. She'd been out of the country limelight for several months, and the song, even without Nelson's rubbery phrasing, was not typical country by any means.

Country Music Hall of Fame historian Paul Kingsbury told National Public Radio in September 2000: "Willie wrote and was writing at that time, early '60s, very different songs from typical country music fare. Instead of the usual three or four chords that were just major chords and sevenths, he was writing 'Crazy' with jazzy minor sevenths, major sevenths, minors."

On top of that, Cline and her brother had been seriously hurt in a car accident just a few months previously, and she wasn't fully recovered when she first recorded the song. Her face was scarred, her hip had been smashed, her wrist was fractured, and she was carryings numerous minor chest injuries. Cline was in the hospital for a month and off the road for nine months before she was well enough to go back to work. But in late August 1961, disobeying doctors' orders, Cline went back to recording with Owen Bradley.

Promotional photograph of Patsy Cline taken in 1961, a short time before her life-threatening car accident.

Bradley, a soulful pianist and clever arranger, had a new sound in his head for country music in general, and Cline and "Crazy" in particular. He wanted to develop a more sophisticated, pop-flavored music that would bring the honky-tonk sound into a more cosmopolitan style, and in doing so find a new and larger audience. He liked the chord changes in Nelson's jazz-tinged song and realized that in Cline he had a singer with the necessary vocal range and emotional flexibility to bring something new to the country table.

So the evening of August 21, 1961, Bradley laid down the instrumental tracks with the cream of Nashville's musicians. Walter Haynes played steel guitar, Harold Bradley played bass, Bob Moore played acoustic bass, Buddy Harman played drums, and Floyd Cramer brought his delicate style to piano. Bradley also brought in Elvis's backing vocalists, the Jordanaires, to add vocal depth to the song. Cline struggled, both with the new sound Bradley was looking for and with her injuries, which prevented her from hitting the high notes without feeling a lot of pain. But a week later, with the backing tracks done and in far better shape physically, Cline had had time to digest the nuances of the song. She was in fine form that night, recording her magnificent vocals in just one take.

Cline was still on crutches a few weeks later when she debuted her new single on the stage of the *Grand Ole Opry* at the Ryman Auditorium. She was imperious, using her powerful but controlled vocals to maximum effect. She received three encores. The song quickly climbed the charts, making it to #2 on the *Billboard* country chart and #9 on the more mainstream pop chart. Most significantly, "Crazy" became a pop music standard, with artists from Linda Ronstadt to the Kidneythieves rock band covering the song over subsequent decades.

OPPOSITE

Faron Young performing on
the *Grand Ole Opry* show
during the 1960s.

"I went in and talked to Hal and I said, 'I found this person—man, he's great. He's a great talent. I think he's a star, and he writes fantastic songs.' And I said, 'Nobody in town wants him or wants his songs, and I think he'd be great. And then I'd have somebody to work with.'"

Such was Cochran's faith in Nelson that when Smith said they'd only take on Nelson by giving the new writer money that had been earmarked for Cochran's upcoming pay raise, Cochran said, "Well, sign him and give him my raise, and do me later or something, because it's gonna help me and everybody here." So they gave him Cochran's $50 raise.

BREAKTHROUGH

As a consequence, sitting in a tiny room at Pamper Music in Goodlettsville, twenty miles outside of Nashville, Nelson was inspired to write "Hello Walls." It was finished in ten minutes, a classic ode to loneliness. Unfortunately, aside from Cochran, many of those who Nelson played the tune to found it more amusing than serious. But one person who didn't was country music legend Faron Young, one of the kingpins of the hardcore Tootsie's crowd, who at the time needed a hit.

Faron Young had been a big star through the 1950s, after coming to prominence on the *Louisiana Hayride* and picking up the nickname the "Singing Sheriff." A solid vocalist, he delivered a smoother version of Hank Williams's and Ernest Tubb's style of '50s honky-tonk.

Aside from hit records, Young also dabbled with a movie career, appearing in around ten films, including *Daniel Boone: Trail Blazer* and *Raiders of Old California*. He was also an astute businessman who invested heavily in Music Row real estate early on and published the trade magazine *Music City News* for many years.

But Faron Young was also a notorious drinker and hellraiser. At times he could be violent and foul mouthed, but he could also be kind, charming, and infinitely generous, especially to new artists like Nelson. He was very much top dog among the revelers at Tootsie's Orchid Lounge.His last big song, "Riverboat," had been more than a year before. When Nelson played him "Hello Walls," Young was intrigued. The song wasn't an obvious a hit, but Young saw its potential, and when Nelson offered to sell it to him, Young declined but loaned the broke songwriter $500 for its use. The song did indeed put Young back at the top of the country charts, where it stayed for nine weeks. When the royalty checks came in, Nelson headed to Tootsie's, where he surprised a seated Faron Young. Young recounted the tale on the *Waylon Jennings and Friends* TV show "He had another check for like $20,000, and I was at Tootsie's, and this arm came around my neck, pulled my mouth open, and he French kissed me."

That success was followed by two more hits written by Nelson, as old Texas pal Billy Walker recorded "Funny How Time Slips Away" and "Crazy" became a smash for Patsy Cline. Also, Ray Price announced plans to record "Night Life."

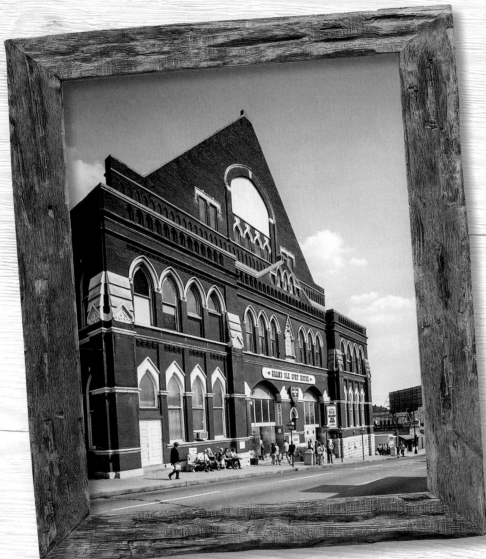

RIGHT

The Ryman Auditorium in Nashville, the former Union Gospel Tabernacle, came to represent the heart of country music as the home of the *Grand Ole Opry* from 1943 to 1974.

Billy Walker had helped Nelson when he was in need of a hand up in the music business, giving him a place to stay in Missouri, providing Nelson with a roof over his head when he first moved to Nashville, and trying to find Willie work on his TV show, the *Ozark Jubilee*. Maybe Walker's own tough beginnings inspired his generosity toward the struggling singer-songwriter.

Walker's mother had died when he was just four years old, leaving him and eight siblings to be raised by their preacher father in depression-hit rural Texas. His father placed Billy in a local orphanage. It was traumatizing, as Walker notes on his website: "He placed me and two of my brothers in the Methodist Orphanage in Waco, Texas. I recall my daddy turning loose of my hand, watching him walk away, and not seeing him again for five years. The orphanage was a cruel place at that time. My brothers and I were isolated for 30 days in one small room. You want to hear about child abuse—they wouldn't be allowed to operate today. I recall one young boy who was made to sleep all night sitting on the commode. They beat us and if we wet the bed, they rubbed our face in it, pulled our hair, made us go without food."

Somehow, despite (or maybe because of) this start in life, Walker forged a music career. In 1949, he won a role on the *Big D Jamboree* radio show in Dallas, which led to a recording deal with Capitol the same year. Through the early 1950s he was a mainstay on the *Louisiana Hayride* in Shreveport, Louisiana, where he gave another new young act a leg up on the career ladder. "In 1955 . . . Elvis joined me for a tour of West Texas. I paid Elvis $150 a day, and $10 car expenses. A young outlaw by the name of Waylon Jennings passed out posters in the town to help promote the show."

Walker moved to Nashville in 1959, joining the *Grand Ole Opry* the following year. A major champion of Willie Nelson's songs, Walker recorded "Funny How Time Slips Away" in 1961, and the track made it to #23 on the *Billboard* country singles chart. It put Walker on the map, and also helped establish Nelson as a writer with serious potential.

BREAKUP

But it wasn't all roses just yet. Nelson was still spending too much money, and often fighting with Martha. Songwriters have to wait a while before they see their royalty money, so with that in mind (and a chance to avoid marital confrontation), Willie talked himself into a gig with Ray Price's band, the Cherokee Cowboys. Price's bass player, Donny Young (who later changed his name to Johnny Paycheck and hit the big time with "Take This Job and Shove It") was leaving, and Price needed a replacement.

Nelson told Ray Waddell at the 2012 *Billboard* Country Music Summit in Nashville: "First of all, Donny Young—or Johnny Paycheck as he'd later call himself—was playing bass for Ray, and he left the band. I was writing songs for Pamper Music, Ray's publishing company. Ray called me and asked me if I could play bass, and I said, 'Well, can't everybody?' So on my way up there on the bus [to meet Price], [steel guitarist] Jimmy Day taught me a few things on the bass. I played guitar and knew the top four strings were very similar. So I had something to go on, and he knew the Ray Price show. By the time I got there, I thought I knew it. Of course, I didn't. I asked Ray years later if he knew I couldn't play bass, and he said, 'Uh huh.'"

Willie Nelson's spell on the road with Price and the Cherokee Cowboys would provide material for barroom tales for years to come. The timing was such that while he was working as a humble $25-a-day musician for Price, the

songwriting royalty checks started coming in. Nelson was not one to save for a rainy day, as he told National Public Radio's *Fresh Air* in 1996: "The faster I made it, the faster I would spend it. Everybody else would travel on the bus, I was still playing bass for Ray Price when 'Hello Walls' made a hit and I got my first royalty check. So I, you know, started flying first class to all the dates as Ray's bass player, right? I'm making $25 a day. And I get a suite at the hotel. Ray's got a regular room at the Holiday Inn, you know, and I got the penthouse."

To top that, Nelson bought Price's top-of-the-range 1959 Cadillac, and gave it to his wife, Martha, to run around Nashville in. Martha and the luxury automobile became well known around town, but the flashy gift and extra cash from Willie's royalty success couldn't save their marriage. The fighting continued, and even when he wasn't on tour, Nelson would increasingly find a reason to stay away from home. Divorce was looming.

LIBERTY RECORDS

Hank Cochran never stopped promoting Nelson, and in the latter part of 1961 persuaded the Liberty Records A&R man to take a listen. Joe Allison, who ran the L.A. office for Liberty, was immediately impressed and saw quality in the songs. Despite Nelson's idiosyncratic vocals, Allison opted to invest in the singer-songwriter. The first single with Liberty was "Mr. Record Man," which received above-average radio play without being a breakthrough record.

Cochran had suggested a well-known female vocalist, Shirley Collie, to complement Nelson's unique sound on record. Allison agreed and brought Shirley and her husband in to the studio in California for some sessions for Nelson's debut solo album, . . . *And Then I Wrote.*

Allison kept it pretty simple with a straightforward country band, instructing them to follow Nelson, not the other way round. At the sessions, which began in August 1961, Willie recorded all his own compositions. Some were downbeat and melancholy like "Crazy," "Darkness on the Face of the Earth," "Funny How Time Slips Away," and "Hello Walls," while others were beer-fueled honky-tonkers including "Undo the Right" (co-written with Cochran) and "Three Days."

His solo single from the album, "Touch Me," went to #7 in May 1962, but that was about it for the debut album after its release in September. Nashville and country music radio wasn't ready yet for Willie Nelson the artist. Songwriter, yes; singer, not yet.

But at that point, Nelson was distracted by a new romance. His marriage with Martha was all but over, and he already had eyes for a new woman, the singer who worked on his debut album, Shirley Collie. For a while the two singers toured with the Ray Price band, before putting their own outfit together with Jimmy Day on steel guitar. Willie and Shirley split the set with their own songs, and Day's glimmering steel complemented both voices perfectly.

The respected rockabilly and swing musician Tommy Allsup produced the 1963 follow-up to . . . *And Then I Wrote*, with seven of its twelve tracks featuring other writers' substandard material. *Here's Willie Nelson* didn't sell well, and although another record was due under his contract, it never saw the light of day. By 1965, the Liberty label was no longer in the country music business, but Nelson wasn't too perturbed as his focus was on the new love of his life, Shirley. Meanwhile Martha, who'd understandably had enough of her husband's cavorting, packed the kids into the Cadillac and drove to Las Vegas to divorce Willie.

Nelson continued to play the road as a trio with Shirley and Jimmy Day, before adding his old Texas pal Johnny Bush (writer of "Whiskey River," later a Nelson concert standard) and settling down in Fort Worth for a short period. Paul English joined the combo on drums, and other guest pickers like Paul Buskirk would play when available. When Shirley Collie's divorce from her husband became final, she and Willie were married. Tired of life on the road, they decided to give music a rest for a while.

HOG FARMER

Nelson found a two-hundred-acre hog farm outside Nashville in Ridgetop, Tennessee, and bought it. It was remote enough for peace and quiet, but Nashville and the music business was a short drive away should he feel the need to reconnect. They signed the papers for the farm on November 22, 1963, the day President Kennedy was assassinated in Dallas.

Johnny Bush helped Nelson run the farm before they hired a farm manager, and, recognizing Willie's newfound stability, Martha sent the kids to live with him and Shirley on the farm. When Martha also found a new love in her life, Mickey Scott, and married him, the new couple bought a home just a mile or so away from the Nelsons' farm.

Compounding family arrangements further, Nelson's father, Ira, and his wife and kids then moved to the farm in Ridgetop, before Nelson's sister, Bobbie, and her husband and three kids likewise settled there. Later Nelson's mother, Myrtle, and her husband moved nearby, while fiddler Wade Ray and drummer Paul English also relocated to the farm with their wives. It was the '60s, after all.

Nelson maintained his Nashville business connection, still writing songs, and briefly had a deal with Monument Records, Roy Orbison's label. But aside from writing a 1963 Christmas smash for Orbison, "Pretty Paper" (which was also a UK hit a year later), the Monument era was largely unproductive.

Country music was in a state of flux in the early 1960s; it needed new blood and a new direction. Nelson was an outsider, and although Nashville musicians recognized his enormous talent, change didn't come easy. Fitting in to a new style that was about to dominate the country airwaves would be the next challenge for Willie Nelson.

✦ Shirley Collie ✦

Willie Nelson first came across wife number two, Shirley Collie, while on the road playing bass with Ray Price. Missouri-born Shirley was well known on the country circuit as a singer, songwriter, and yodeler. The flame-haired firebrand had worked with Red Foley on the *Ozark Jubilee* television show. She traveled the road with the touring *Philip Morris Country Music Show*, where she met her husband, DJ Bill Collie, who was the show's host. Full of personality, Shirley even won a role on the Groucho Marx TV show *You Bet Your Life*, and in 1962 would decline the role of Pearl Bodine in the TV series *The Beverly Hillbillies*, to go on the road with Willie.

Collie signed to Liberty Records in California in 1960, and charted with the Harlan Howard song "Dime a Dozen," which made the Top 30 of the *Billboard* country chart in 1962. She also made #23 on the same chart with a duet with Warren Smith, "Why Baby Why," previously a big hit for George Jones.

Producer Joe Allison and songwriter Hank Cochran were both fans of Collie's singing, and, convinced that her style would suit Willie Nelson's, put them together in the studio for Willie's first album. Recorded in August 1963 at the Radio Recorders studios in Los Angeles, their voices blended remarkably well, and the fact that the two were essentially falling in love during the sessions made the music all the more authentic and emotional.

In November 1963, Allison recorded Nelson again, this time at Bradley's Barn—literally a barn outside Nashville converted to a recording studio by Owen

Shirley Collie in 1962, as she hit the country charts with "Willingly."

Bradley. Willie Nelson and Shirley Collie sang, while top session players Bob Moore, Pig Robbins, Ray Edenton, and Jimmy Day backed the lovers in the studio. The combination worked, and Liberty released the duet "Willingly" as a single in March 1962. It slowly rose to the #10 spot by August of that year.

Nelson's own Liberty Records debut single, "The Part Where I Cry," backed with "Mr. Record Man," had been a success only in Texas, failing to make the *Billboard* charts. It was after his breakthrough with Collie on "Willingly" that Nelson's next single, "Touch Me," made it to #7.

. . . And Then I Wrote

SIDE ONE

Touch Me ✴ Wake Me When It's Over ✴
Hello Walls ✴ Funny How Time Slips Away
✴ Crazy ✴ The Part Where I Cry

SIDE TWO

Mr. Record Man ✴ Three Days ✴ One Step
Beyond ✴ Undo the Right ✴ Darkness on the
Face of the Earth ✴ Where My House Lives

RECORDED

August 22–23, September 11–12, 1962

RELEASED

September 1962

LABEL

Liberty

PERSONNEL

Willie Nelson (guitar, vocals) ✴ Shirley
Collie (guitar, vocals)

PRODUCER

Joe Allison

Willie Nelson's debut album, . . . *And Then I Wrote*, was aptly titled, given that it was Nelson's success as a Nashville songwriter that saw him signed to Liberty Records in the first place. For Nelson it was a natural progression from songwriter to recording artist, but while the album, in retrospect, is way above average, the country music scene at the time wasn't quite ready for Nelson's idiosyncratic vocal and performing style.

Joe Allison was a DJ turned songwriter. In 1959, Joe and his wife, Audrey, had written "He'll Have to Go," a multimillion-selling global hit for country crooner Jim Reeves. By the early 1960s, Joe was also producing records for the Liberty label—just as the company had set up a country division in Nashville. Allison sensed Nelson had what it took to progress from writer to performer and sent him into Quonset Hut studio on Music Row, where he recorded at an all-night session that went through August 22 and 23, 1961. The tracks produced that night included "Touch Me" and "The Part Where I Cry," which were also earmarked as the top and flipside of his debut single for the label. Further sessions were booked in September at the Liberty studios in Los Angeles, where Willie cut "Crazy," "Darkness on the Face of the Earth," "Three Days," "Funny How Times Slips Away," "Mr. Record Man," and "Hello Walls." When "Touch Me" was released as a single, it made the top ten of the *Billboard* Hot Country Singles chart in May 1962.

THE NASHVILLE SOUND

As country music entered the 1960s, the industry was reeling from the rockabilly rock-and-roll explosion that had boomed out of Memphis in the mid-1950s. The classic honky-tonk sound of Hank Williams and Ernest Tubb seemed staid and dated in contrast to Carl Perkins, Elvis Presley, Johnny Cash, and Jerry Lee Lewis, the quartet of Sun Records acts who changed pop forever.

Country music sales dipped, and many radio stations switched formats, from country to rock-and-roll. Ray Price was king of the honky-tonk circuit through the 1950s, but by the turn of the 1960s he could see that a new direction was necessary in Nashville. He told WHYY's *Fresh Air* on National Public Radio in 1999 that producers in Nashville had to come up with a way to broaden country's

BELOW

Willie Nelson (far right) having just signed with Monument Records in early 1964. Monument boss Fred Foster is at center, and at left is another new signee, singer and guitarist Fred Carter.

BELOW

Willie signs his contract with
RCA Records in Nashville,
November 24, 1964.

audience. "They had to do something to kind of fix it, where the people that listened to the Tony Bennetts and the Frank Sinatras, those people would like the song or the music."

One producer in particular played a significant role in creating an alternative country music style, one that employed layered backing vocals and strings, and would become known around the world as the Nashville Sound. That producer was a session guitarist turned record company executive at the all-powerful RCA Records by the name of Chet Atkins.

Speaking to me in 1990 from his office on Nashville's Music Row, Atkins was humble about his own part in changing country music's direction. "I was a musician who had been educated in music, and I knew how to produce records. You have to remember that in the '50s they didn't really have producers. I mean, I produced songs for Elvis, but there was no producer credit on the records back then. It was a different world. But everyone in the business in Nashville recognized that something different was needed, so I tried a different approach with a more pop sound that we hoped would appeal to the country fans and new pop fans, and initially the artists liked it too."

Atkins knew that Willie Nelson was good, and felt he had both the jazzy intonation in his vocals and sophisticated songs to break through into a country-pop format. "I knew he'd make it, just didn't know when!"

"I TRIED A DIFFERENT APPROACH WITH A MORE POP SOUND THAT WE HOPED WOULD APPEAL TO THE COUNTRY FANS AND NEW POP FANS, AND INITIALLY THE ARTISTS LIKED IT TOO."

—CHET ATKINS

He signed Nelson in 1964, the same year Willie was finally asked to perform on the *Grand Ole Opry*. That didn't last long because in the 1960s the *Opry* insisted that its members played at least twenty-six shows every year. Those were prime weekend gig opportunities for road warriors like Nelson, and after a year he quit, refusing to be restricted by the *Opry*'s 26-concert rules. He also became a regular on the Nashville-produced *Ernest Tubb Show* on television, which launched in 1965. "It was a lot of fun," Willie recalled to Bill DeYoung for *Goldmine* magazine in February 1999. "That was back when Jack Greene was playing drums in the *Ernest Tubb Show* . . . I helped him host a little bit along, but he was the master of ceremonies."

While TV was fun, recording with Chet Atkins would be interesting and challenging, but would prove to be ultimately frustrating.

3

1969 ✦ 1981

Stardust

BELOW

Top session guitarist Grady Martin, a member of the exclusive group of studio musicians known as the Nashville A-Team.

Nelson was delighted to be working with two such acclaimed guitarists as producer Chet Atkins and main guitar session man Grady Martin at the same time. Atkins was convinced that Nelson's unique sound and vocal delivery gave him the ingredients necessary to break through into the mainstream. "Willie was just so good, I honestly believed we'd make a pile of money! Maybe he was just ahead of his time. I don't really know," Atkins told me in 1990.

Success and fame at RCA Records wasn't to be. The first few albums and singles made only minor inroads into the charts. Between 1966 and 1969 his best singles placings were #19 with "One in a Row," and #13 for "Bring Me Sunshine."

Despite good intentions, Atkins couldn't get the mix right for Willie Nelson. He later passed the production reins to Elvis producer Felton Jarvis, who added more syrup to the pie and, in retrospect, clogged Nelson's artistry even further.

Kris Kristofferson, a good pal of Nelson's in the mid-1960s, saw what was happening—or, more correctly, not happening—for Willie and Chet Atkins, as he told *Texas Monthly* in 2008: "In Nashville they didn't understand that he didn't sound like every other country singer. We thought he was like a jazz singer, someone who never did sing on the beat like most people did. And I remember trying to explain to people who Willie was, and they just didn't appreciate him yet. I can remember even my publisher said, 'Willie can't sing.' Fortunately, Willie never felt that way."

Looking back in June 2010, Nelson told Parade.com, "I didn't feel like I failed in Nashville. I felt like they failed to realize that I really knew what I was talking about. I was writing some pretty good songs and my singing wasn't that bad. I had a base in Texas. But the majority of the people that I recorded for, and the publishing companies that I wrote for, had heard stories about how popular I was in Texas. But they never left their desks in Nashville long enough to come by and check it out. Whenever I'd go down to Texas to play to thousands of people on the weekend, they didn't know anything about it in Nashville. So it was a big disconnect between Nashville and the rest of the world for me back in those days. So I felt like I had to go back out of Nashville in order to make those connections again."

ON THE ROAD

While RCA labored unsuccessfully to set Nelson's career on fire, Willie took matters into his own hands again and looked into playing more live dates. Traveling was a tough part of playing on the road in the '60s. Before he could afford to rent or buy a tour bus, Willie's band traveled in assorted station wagons, cars, and a trailer attached to his automobile. But getting paid could be even tougher.

Fortunately, Nelson's drummer, Paul English, took care of any serious disputes with club owners and booking agents. Willie first met Paul English when he was DJ at KNAC in Fort Worth, through Paul's guitarist brother Oliver English. In the '50s, Paul made no pretense of being a professional-class drummer, but he had a natural sense of rhythm and by 1966 had acquired a technique good enough to drum for Willie Nelson. And so he did, a move that probably saved his life, as he explained to Savingcountrymusic.com, in 2009: "I started making the papers in 1956 when the *Fort Worth Press* started running a '10 Most Unwanted' list. I made it five years in a row. I was involved in three murder trials, but they never led to anything. I was the kind of guy they were always trying to stick charges on. . . . In '55 I started running girls. This went on for a long time. It was a good business but you had to work hard. . . . I had become

OPPOSITE

Left to right: Willie Nelson, promoter Crash Stewart, and road manager Gino McCoslin in 1966, when Willie put together a country music package tour for Stewart.

really adept at picking locks. We had a contest on how many daytime burglaries we could pull and I think I pulled twelve. I don't think I was ever legitimate until I started playing drums for Willie in 1966."

In the tough club scene, Willie wasn't one to back down from a fight, either. Self-protection was key, as he told David Sheff for *Playboy* magazine in November 2002: "I played around when I was pretty young, playing some of the roughest joints anywhere. The best was the Bloody Bucket in West Texas when we carried pistols in our guitar cases." When Willie was drinking, which he typically was in the 1950s and '60s, he had a fearsome temper. Indeed, as Willie told Bill DeYoung in *Goldmine* magazine, it was to calm that frequent rage that Paul English encouraged Nelson to find peace of mind with marijuana, which Willie had been dabbling with since first puffing on the weed in Texas in 1954.

"I PLAYED AROUND WHEN I WAS PRETTY YOUNG, PLAYING SOME OF THE ROUGHEST JOINTS ANYWHERE. THE BEST WAS THE BLOODY BUCKET IN WEST TEXAS WHEN WE CARRIED PISTOLS IN OUR GUITAR CASES." —WILLIE NELSON

At a road show in Phoenix, Arizona, Nelson got talking to another young country music singer, Waylon Jennings, from Lubbock, Texas. Nelson was playing the Riverside Ballroom and had heard about Jennings, who had a regular gig at the nearby JD's club. Backstage, Jennings told Nelson he felt the two Texans were musically connected. Jennings, like Willie, worked occasionally as a DJ before getting onstage as a musician; in Jennings's case, as bass player with rock-and-roll pioneer Buddy Holly. He famously gave up his seat to the Big Bopper on that fateful last flight that Buddy Holly and the band took in the winter of 1959.

Waylon peppered Nelson with questions about Nashville, since he was ready to get out of Phoenix and hit the big time himself. Nelson advised him that, from his own experience, Music City was not kind to musically opinionated nonconformists like himself and Waylon. Contrary to the core, within months Jennings had moved to Nashville and been signed by producer Chet Atkins to RCA Records. They had no idea then, in 1966, that both Nelson and Jennings would have plenty of on-the-road adventures in the coming years and change the face of country music around the globe.

In mid-1966, when Ray Price opted out of a tour that promoter Crash Stewart was putting together, Nelson jumped at the chance to put together a package show of several artists himself. Nelson wasn't a name draw at that point, so he pulled in Marty Robbins as a star attraction and added Hank Cochran, Johnny Bush, and Stonewall Jackson to the package—plus a new young act named Charley Pride, an African American singer originally from Mississippi. Stewart was instructed by Willie to book the dates, getting himself and the others $400 a night during the week, $500 on Fridays nights, and $600 a night on weekends.

COUNTRY PRIDE

Nelson took a sizable risk with Charley Pride. Bookers and club owners who dealt primarily with country music were mostly opposed to booking a black singer in the mid-'60s American South. The fight for Civil Rights was at its height, and despite the Civil Rights Act of 1964, much of the United States, especially in the South, was still in effect segregated.

Although country music had embraced a black artist before—harmonic player DeFord Bailey, for instance, appeared regularly on the *Grand Ole Opry* back in the 1920s—the format was predominantly white and conservative. But within that prejudice, there was a good deal of second-guessing involved. Even more liberally minded club managers and promoters tended to presume that white artists, customers, and fans would not accept artists of color playing country music.

The fact is that many musicians like Willie Nelson and Chet Atkins, and even Pride's first manager, Jack Johnson, saw beyond race and recognized an incredible voice and performing talent. Pride himself is convinced that music fans were always receptive to his music, despite his color. He told the *Houston Press* on April 25, 2012, "People never believe me, but in my entire career, I've never heard one hoot from the audience that was meant in any kind of negative way. It wasn't country music fans that resisted me, it was the promoters and club owners who always had a reason to not book me when we were getting started."

Charley Pride, one of eleven children of sharecroppers Mack and Tessie Pride, initially escaped Mississippi poverty by excelling as a baseball star for the Memphis Red Sox, part of the Negro American League. Pride entertained his teammates on long bus trips, singing and playing. Initially, baseball was his career dream, but after being turned down by the New York Mets, Pride headed to Nashville. Coincidentally Nashville manager/agent Jack Johnson had decided to look for a black country act.

Jack Johnson pitched Pride's music around Nashville's movers and shakers; most reactions were negative, but there was one interested response. Former Sun Records engineer "Cowboy" Jack Clement was now a freelance Nashville producer, and decided to cut some tracks for Charley Pride. Clement told *No Depression* magazine in August 2004, "I had a session set up at RCA Studio B and we went in

OPPOSITE

Willie onstage in May 1970, at the Palomino Club, Los Angeles, one of the many venues he played on the rowdy club and bar circuit. Willie is playing his regular guitar "Trigger," the Martin N-20 that he'd acquired the year before, and would later be lavishly decorated with inscriptions by fellow singers and musicians.

and did it. I paid for it, and . . . well, then I had the only Charley Pride record in town. I had this office with these big speakers, and I'd get people in there and play Charley's record. Loud, man. Like, really loud. I'd play that record and then I'd show 'em his picture. That was fun."

Talking to Clement in his Jack's Tracks studios in Nashville in 1990, he told me, "It was like a reverse of what happened with Elvis, when everybody though Elvis was a black guy singing R&B. They all thought Charley was a white guy with a hell of a voice. Chet Atkins was so impressed he signed him to RCA. And then you know, Willie Nelson, who never did think like the rest of the crowd, took him on the road."

Atkins initially wondered how to market the new singer, given his color. RCA opted for sending out singles without any photos. "We figured if they just listened to how good the music was, once they found out Charley wasn't white they'd love him anyhow," Atkins told me in 1990. In 1967, his single "Just between You and Me" went Top 10 on the *Billboard* country chart, and Pride became a mainstream country music star almost overnight. But prior to that, when free-thinking Nelson offered him a slot on the road, Pride's race was a crucial issue, and a potentially dangerous one at that.

Back in 1966, the Long Horn Ballroom in Dallas, established by Bob Wills for hardcore country music, was switching its demographics a little, and had Sunday and Monday nights set aside for black artists and black audiences. It was strictly segregated.

One night Nelson was playing the honky-tonk and called up Charley from backstage. The club owner wasn't happy, and the audience made their own displeasure clear until Nelson walked up to Pride and kissed him full on the mouth. With that, Pride launched into his song "The Snakes Crawl at Night," which won over the crowd immediately.

Nelson remembers the night well, as he told *Parade Magazine* in 2010. "He'd been treated unfairly. They didn't want him to sing there. And the owner of the club, who's a real good friend of mine, was a solid redneck, and he didn't want him there. So I kissed Charlie on the mouth. I was just trying to ease the tensions a little bit."

To this day Pride keeps a picture that Willie gave him many a year ago. On it is handwritten: "To the next No. 1 country singer, Charley Pride. Your friend, Willie Nelson."

CONNIE

Lackluster promotion of his records and continuous road gigs (albeit financially successful) were putting a strain on Willie's family life. It may have been the era of hippies and communes, but his own extended family situation in Ridgetop was far from harmonious. His son Billy was never happy with Willie's new wife, Shirley, while Susie and Lana rebelled in their own ways. Willie had numerous infidelities while on the road. One night in Texas he asked a particularly attractive blond woman for her phone number. They hooked up the next time he was in Houston and began an affair, as Connie Koepke would recall in *People* magazine in 1980.

The infidelity came out in the open in 1969, when Shirley opened a bill from a Houston hospital that concerned the birth of a Paula Carlene to "Willie and Connie Nelson." Shirley left, divorce proceedings started, and Connie moved into Ridgetop. Connie and Willie were married before the divorce was finalized.

On December 23, 1969, Willie was at a Christmas party in Nashville when he received a message that his home at Ridgetop was on fire. Getting there as quickly as possible, the singer boldy dashed inside: "By the time I got there, it was burning

real good," he told *People* magazine in 1980, "but I had this pound of Colombian grass inside. I wasn't being brave running in there to get my dope—I was trying to keep the firemen from finding it, and turning me over to the police."

The Nelson clan was temporarily homeless while the farm was repaired, and as he made good money playing live in Texas, they relocated to the Lone Star State—temporarily at first, making their base at an old dude ranch in Bandera, a few miles outside San Antonio.

COUNTER-COUNTRY

Texas gave Nelson the space and time to reconsider his life and career. He was newly married and decided to finally quit drinking, as he explained to the *New York Times* in 2012. He didn't like the temperamental rage that alcohol induced in him. In keeping with the times, Willie Nelson gravitated more toward marijuana for relaxation and recreation, maybe even inspiration. Significantly, weed was the drug of choice for the hippie counterculture, a community Nelson was increasingly intrigued by and empathetic toward. Meanwhile, Willie still had to figure out where his place was, if anywhere, in country music's spiritual home of Nashville, Tennessee.

Country music, by the late '60s and early '70s, had become far removed from the dynamic, earthy music of Hank Williams, Bill Monroe, Bob Wills, and Ernest Tubb. The sound was increasingly sweet and poppy, and the sophisticated Nashville Sound initiated by Owen Bradley and Chet Atkins a decade before had blossomed under hot producers like Billy Sherrill, who cut traditional country instrumentation from many of his records and instead added lush string sections. In fact, to many of the artists who worked there, Nashville seemed stuck in the past—especially to younger performers, who were hugely influenced by their rock-and-roll counterparts.

Country and bluegrass guitarist Norman Blake recalled, in 2012: "It was a very loose time, and the counterculture was in flower, too. There were a lot of folks moving to town and the young people back then were into all the same things that they were on the West Coast. And there was a culture clash, because the new pickers wanted more freedom, more artistic license to experiment and create new sounds. But Nashville was an industry town run by a small group of people, so there were cliques and power games going on for sure."

The lines between rock, pop, and country were being increasingly blurred. Country artists like Nelson, Jennings, Bobby Bare, Mickey Newbury, and Kris Kristofferson were inspired by what they saw happening in rock-and-roll, from the Beatles' experimentation to the spirit of hippie community at festivals like Monterey Pop and Woodstock. They were envious of the musical abandon and power enjoyed by acts like Led Zeppelin, Lynyrd Skynyrd, the Stones, the Who, and the Allman Brothers. Simultaneously, both rock and pop acts, including the Byrds, Mike Nesmith of the Monkees, and notably Bob Dylan, played and recorded in Nashville, developing a country-rock genre that would explode with California band the Eagles in 1972.

But Nashville still represented a very conservative music industry, the business running as a slick and highly structured machine. Record company bosses like Chet Atkins and Billy Sherrill doubled as producers. Producers hired musicians from a select list, an A team of session players who performed on most major label recordings—these were professionals, who recorded fast in three-hour blocks. Being a session musician was essentially a nine-to-five job, with a

OPPOSITE

Willie on stage with Emmylou Harris and Joan Baez at the Circle Star Theatre in Palo Alto, California, in 1974. Emmylou (center) in particular was another example of the crossover from traditional folk-oriented music to the country and country-rock markets.

OPPOSITE

Willie Nelson opening his
annual 4th of July Picnic
in 1974, before a crowd
of over 50,000, in
College Station, Texas.

concomitant clock in, clock out mentality. The musicians did what the producer told them, with little or no interaction with songwriters or artists. And once the producer's chosen songs were recorded, the record company selected which songs would make singles, and in what order those singles would be released.

Artists like Kristofferson, Jennings, and Nelson felt constrained from exploring the depths of a song and being forced to record three or four tracks in a three-hour session. For most old school *Opry* acts, the system worked perfectly. But the new breed, raised on a diet of British rock, traditional country, folk, and blues—and familiar with the looser setup in other centers of the recording industry—were not happy.

WAYLON

Frustration was the order of the day. Waylon Jennings found some success within the RCA system—his first Top 10 single, "(That's What You Get) For Lovin' Me," came in 1966, and he scored a #2 with "Only Daddy That'll Walk the Line" in '68—but it came with the price of a rocky relationship with Chet Atkins and the company.

Admittedly, Jennings's use of amphetamines, especially when he shared a room with Johnny Cash in north Nashville in 1966, didn't help his cause. With records not selling in substantial numbers, Jennings toured to make money, but like Nelson, he always seemed to be struggling to show a profit. The wild road lifestyle calmed a shade in 1969 when he married his fourth wife and love of his life, singer Jessi Colter, but as his musical and artistic frustrations grew, so did his drug use. It was a vicious circle, his strung-out behavior hardly winning sympathy with the executives at RCA or in the wider Nashville music business community.

Waylon's long-time drummer and good friend Richie Albright knew of a New York lawyer/manager who he felt could fight in Waylon's corner when it came to business. The record industry was changing, in rock-and-roll at least, with aggressive young agents and managers refusing to let record companies screw over their artists. But not so in country music. Jennings wasn't initially ready to sign with an outsider, but after a bout of hepatitis and a long period of time off the road, he asked RCA for a small advance to tide him over. Their only offer was to lock him into a long-term contract, which Jennings refused, turning instead to Albright's recommendation. The man in

question was New York–based Neil Reshen, a man who would play key roles in both Waylon and Willie Nelson's careers in the 1970s.

Reshen had started in the business doing tax accounting for RCA Records president Ken Glancy and the jazz icon Miles Davis, which led to his managing Davis and other high-profile clients. Reshen was fearless and went head-to-head with RCA's top brass in New York to secure an impressive new contract for Jennings, guaranteeing him not only more money but also artistic control. Jennings responded with a string of albums in 1973 in which he began to find his

BELOW

A portrait of Tompall Glaser, who founded the Glaser Sound Studio—dubbed "Hillbilly Central" by a New York journalist—in 1969.

own voice. He spent hours working through the night in the studio, and the results were obvious to all. Given time, Jennings was a genuine artist.

In 1972, before his RCA contract was successfully renegotiated, the company released Waylon's album *Ladies Love Outlaws*, which was one of the first real outlaw-themed country albums and a reasonable seller. After being given full creative control, Jennings was now able to fully embrace his maverick spirit, and he made his mark with two subsequent albums in 1973, *Lonesome, On'ry and Mean* and *Honky Tonk Heroes*.

Two more hit albums followed in 1974. *This Time* topped the *Billboard* country chart, with its title track Waylon's first #1 country single, and the title track from the follow-up *Ramblin' Man* likewise made #1. Then in 1975, the #1 single "Are

You Sure Hank Done It This Way" helped make *Dreaming My Dreams* Jennings's first gold album.

The catalyst for Jennings, and indeed what would turn into the so-called outlaw movement, was a Nashville recording studio nicknamed "Hillbilly Central," officially the Glaser Sound Studio. The studio was opened by Tompall Glaser, an artist (with the Glaser Brothers) and music publisher, who plowed publishing money into a studio for what he saw as a new wave of like-minded artists who wanted out of the rigid Nashville recording dogma.

There was no nine-to five-mentality at Hillbilly Central. Artists and musicians adopted the ways of their rock-and-roll cousins and recorded through the night if they so wished. Jennings was inspired by the freedom, and more and more like-minded maverick artists made Hillbilly Central their home, among them Bobby Bare, Jessi Colter, John Hartford, Shel Silverstein, and of course Willie Nelson, when he was in Nashville. Glaser hired a publicist, Hazel Smith, who when asked by a journalist what kind of music was going down at Hillbilly Central came up with the term "outlaw." On CMT's *American Revolutions: Wanted the Outlaws* documentary she said, "I turned to an old blue collegiate dictionary, and I found at the very bottom the definition that said 'living on the outside of the written law,' and I thought, 'Well, ****, that's what they are doing!'"

"I TURNED TO AN OLD BLUE COLLEGIATE DICTIONARY, AND I FOUND AT THE VERY BOTTOM THE DEFINITION THAT SAID 'LIVING ON THE OUTSIDE OF THE WRITTEN LAW,' AND I THOUGHT, 'WELL, ****, THAT'S WHAT THEY ARE DOING!'" —HAZEL SMITH

AUSTIN

While Jennings, with Reshen's help, fought the Nashville system from within, Willie Nelson was taking a sabbatical from Tennessee to enjoy life in the dusty wide-open spaces of Texas. His latest album for RCA, *Yesterday's Wine*, featured some fine, introspective moments, featuring Nelson the troubadour, as opposed to Nelson the hot songwriter. In his autobiography, Willie said RCA was

FOLLOWING PAGES
Willie and Waylon enjoying a drink together in New York City, 1978.

unimpressed, convinced that Nelson had either outgrown or lost interest in his country music fan base. So instead of moving back to the repaired and restored farm in Tennessee, Nelson stayed in Texas—not Houston, as he had originally considered, but Austin. Austin was a beautiful city. It had a top university, which guaranteed a young demographic, and was remarkably open-minded and nonjudgmental.

Nelson's sister, Bobbie, had already moved down there. After a spell in a downtown apartment, Nelson and his family—with Connie now pregnant—found a home in the countryside, just outside the city.

Delighted with the crowd's reactions down in Texas, Nelson persuaded his old friend Waylon to play the rowdy young redneck and hippie audiences in Austin. Jennings would recall how on the first night he played a gig there, he said onstage to drummer Richie Albright, "Somebody go get that little redheaded son of a bitch. What's he got me into?"

With a burgeoning fan base that now included a large element drawn from the student community, in March 1972 Nelson played on the final day of the three-day Dripping Springs Reunion festival. "When Woodstock happened," he told *Texas Monthly* in April 2012, "I saw all those folks come together to listen to all kinds of music. I decided that would be a good thing to do around Austin." The following year Nelson revived the spirit of the festival, with the first of his annual 4th of July Picnics. That first picnic, also held in Dripping Springs, featured Willie, Waylon, Kris Kristofferson, John Prine, Tom T. Hall, and Doug Sahm.

After a sensational concert in August 1972 at the recently opened Armadillo World Headquarters (which would be Austin's flagship rock venue in the early '70s), Nelson decided that it was time to take charge of his career again. One night he drove into town to see his old pal Waylon play the Armadillo; Jennings enthused about his new manager, Neil Reshen, who had renegotiated his RCA contract. Nelson was intrigued and liked the idea of having someone tough to deal with executives, so he also signed with Reshen. Temporarily, at least, it was a good decision.

The New York manager reputedly negotiated a $25,000-a-year deal with Atlantic Records, where Willie was the label's first-ever country signing. Unlike RCA Records, Atlantic Records, formed by brothers Nesuhi and Ahmet Ertegun in 1947, had no history of or interest in country music per se, at least not until 1972, when their vice president, Jerry Wexler, signed Willie Nelson. Wexler appreciated Nelson's idiosyncratic vocal style, likening him to Ray Charles (who back in the '50s was the label's biggest star) instead of complaining that he didn't sound like Jim Reeves or Faron Young.

The first album on Atlantic, *Shotgun Willie*, won rave reviews when released in May 1973, and sold better than anything Nelson had recorded on RCA. The album featured the original lineup of what would become his regular backing band, the Family, comprising sister Bobbie on piano, Mickey Raphael on harmonica, drummer Paul English, guitarist Jody Payne, and Bee Spears on bass.

SHOTGUN WILLIE

Pop music was in a state of change. Country rock was flying high out on the West Coast with a countrified rock band called the Eagles. Bob Dylan had been dabbling with country, while southern rock–meets–country acts such as the Allman Brothers and Lynyrd Skynyrd were playing to fans that loved both country and rock-and-roll. And significantly, Atlantic had enjoyed a smash with Crosby, Stills, Nash & Young's folk rock masterpiece *Déjà Vu* in 1970. Wexler, a former *Billboard* reporter (who is credited with coining the term "rhythm and blues"), had a background in soul music and pop. He had produced numerous

ABOVE

The Allman Brothers, one of the emerging southern rock acts who appealed to both rock and country fans in the 1970s.

classic tracks, including "Shake, Rattle and Roll" by Big Joe Turner, Ray Charles's "What'd I Say," and Aretha Franklin's "(You Make Me Feel Like) A Natural Woman." But although Willie was essentially a song man at that stage, and Wexler understood his abilities as a writer, the producer was also a fan of his nonconformist vocal style.

Wexler told *Texas Monthly* in 2008, "The three masters of rubato in our age are Frank Sinatra, Ray Charles, and Willie Nelson . . . the art of gliding over the meter and extending it until you think they're going to miss the next actual musical demarcation—but they always arrive there, at bar one. It's some kind of musical miracle."

Aware of Nelson's many frustrations during his RCA years, Wexler promised Willie complete studio control and artistic freedom if he signed with Atlantic's new country music division. Atlantic opened a Nashville office in 1972 under Rick Sabjek, and alongside Nelson, Wexler signed Doug Sahm, John Prine, and Henson Cargill.

Nelson traveled to New York to record the sessions that would become the album *Shotgun Willie.* It was a sterner, harder album than his last for RCA, and the title track, reflecting Nelson's recently acquired nickname, had its origins in a tale that could have easily ended Nelson's life and career.

Nelson's daughter Lana, just like his own mother, had fallen in love at a young age and was married to a young man named S. Willie recounts in his autobiography that when he learned that S. had assaulted his daughter, he jumped into his truck, quickly drove over to Lana's home nearby, and gave his son-in-law a couple of good slaps and a stern warning of what would happen if he touched his daughter again.

Later, S. and his brothers paid Willie a visit at his Ridgetop home and reportedly fired guns at Nelson. The bullets just missed. Nelson and drummer Paul English grabbed their M1 rifles and shot back at S.'s truck. Lana later confirmed that S. had taken Nelson's grandson, Nelson Ray, and that he planned on taking Willie out. Prepared for trouble, Nelson and tough guy English laid in wait, and when the brothers drove up to Nelson's home, both Willie and English peppered their truck with shells from their shotguns till the trespassers drove off. S. calmed down and came to the farm to apologize the following day. English told him he was just pleased that S. had driven away that day because, as he told Nick Patoski of *Oxford American* in 2015: "Otherwise, I would've had to aim to kill, rather than shoot to miss."

Excited to be in New York with Wexler, Nelson wrote the title track while in the Big Apple, as he recalled for Atlantic Records' *The Atlantic Sessions* booklet: "I walked out of the studio and back to my hotel. In my room I paced from corner to corner, listening to radio waves, the old sensation surging through me. Then I went to the bathroom and sat down. I saw a sanitary napkin envelope in the sink. I picked it up and started writing."

Jerry Wexler, Arif Mardin, and David Briggs produced Willie's New York tracks, and the album chosen as his debut for Atlantic was very much a prototype

for the unbridled free-form Nelson that would emerge via the outlaw movement over the next few years. The album was not a huge seller, but it brought Nelson a new and hip young audience.

Rolling Stone was quick to praise the new Willie Nelson: "At the age of 39, Nelson finally seems destined for the stardom he deserves….Willie Nelson's roots lie in blues and gospel as well as in country, and his music rightfully belongs within the ever-widening spectrum of pop."

Nelson embraced the Texas lifestyle, relating more and more to the hippie counterculture that was prevalent in Austin. He relaxed, let his hair grow, stopped shaving, and adopted an "outlaw" western look. "I noticed that everyone dressed very comfortably, wearing jeans and tennis shoes and T-shirts, and every time I showed up in a suit and tie, I felt a bit out of place," he told the UK's *Guardian* newspaper in 2015. "I felt like I was out-dressing my audience, so I decided to make it easier on me and dress the way they dressed. It was the way I had dressed all my life, anyway—T-shirts and blue jeans—so it was an easy change to make." It was the beginning of the bandana, beard, and braids look that would be his signature sartorial style ever after.

RED HEADED STRANGER

Willie Nelson was back home, and his new music reflected the change. His work with Jerry Wexler at Atlantic Records showcased a new Willie—a mix of the clean-cut professional songwriter and signs of the devil-may-care troubadour that would emerge over the next few years. Just as Waylon Jennings had found his voice, so now did Nelson.

Unfortunately, the Atlantic Records journey would come to an end when the label closed its Nashville country music division in 1975. Trusting fellow maverick Waylon's judgment in choice of manager, Nelson asked Neil Reshen, Waylon's manager, to look after his affairs and score him a new record deal.

Reshen was not cut from the same cloth as most Nashville country music managers. Their approach was old school, and negotiating was done with an air of southern gentility. But Reshen was a New Yorker, brash and fast-talking, and he knew how to get want he needed for his artist. If the Eagles had David Geffen and Irving Azoff, and Led Zeppelin had Peter Grant, then country acts—if they ever wanted to join the rock-and-roll big time—needed more bite and muscle around the boardroom tables. Reshen called Columbia's president, Bruce Lundvall, and got Nelson a pile of cash in advance and the right to total creative freedom.

Nelson's two Atlantic albums, *Shotgun Willie* and *Phases and Stages*, had bridged the gap between the Nashville sound Nelson and the outlaw Nelson that emerged in Texas in the mid '70s, but still retained much of the overlush production that disguised Willie's true musical character for years. But by talking his affection for concept albums (*Phases and Sages* was a concept album about divorce) to the

WILLIE NELSON
RED HEADED STRANGER

R.H.S. Productions & Pangaea in association with Wrangler Jeans present
A Willie Nelson/Bill Wittliff Production of Red Headed Stranger
Starring WILLIE NELSON   MORGAN FAIRCHILD   R.G. ARMSTRONG
ROYAL DANO & KATHARINE ROSS as LAURIE   Produced by WILLIE NELSON & BILL WITTLIFF
Associate Producers DAVID ANDERSON   ETHEL VOSGITEL & BARRY FEY
Director of Photography NEIL ROACH   Original Music by WILLIE NELSON
Written & Directed by BILL WITTLIFF
© 1986 Red Headed Stranger
Ltd. All Rights Reserved.   An Alive Films Release

Wrangler

old West, Nelson found his voice, complete with sagebrush guitar, lonesome echo-heavy production, and minimal instrumentation. The album centered on an old Western song, "Red Headed Stranger," which Willie Nelson had sung in his early days as a DJ. Nelson then conjured up a backstory that went before the title song. The daring concept album focused on a man who murders a cheating wife and lover, and ends up on the run. The record features Nelson originals mixed with country covers, and moved along with western movie–style narration.

Instead of recording in Nashville or New York with a top producer, Nelson recorded the songs for the Columbia album himself in a small studio in Garland, Texas, for less than $20,000. He hired an engineer, Phi York, and played wonderful spacey guitar on his pet instrument, Trigger, alongside just bass, drums, mandolin, harmonica (the esteemed Mickey Raphael), and sister Bobbie on keys. It was recorded fast, unplugged so to speak, and performed live as much as possible.

OPPOSITE

Poster for the movie of *Red Headed Stranger*, starring Willie Nelson and Morgan Fairchild, and released in 1986.

"YOU GO IN THERE WITH A SMALL BUDGET, NOBODY GETS TO CUT UP A LOT OF MONEY. IF YOU GO IN WITH A MILLION-DOLLAR BUDGET, THEN EVERYBODY MAKES A LITTLE, BUT THE MUSIC MAY NOT BE THAT GREAT." —WILLIE NELSON

When Nelson played the results to Columbia executive Bruce Lundvall, the record company man was horrified. The tracks were basic and very simply recorded, the instrumentation was laid back and minimal, and there was an overall sense of the recording being nothing more than a first-time demo of the album. But Nelson was convinced he'd finally found his voice. Good friend Waylon Jennings stepped in and demanded that the label leave the music to Willie, while Columbia delayed the release. Possibly perturbed that Nelson spent so little money on the project, Lundvall was hesitant in making a decision.

"We were determined to play our music mainly the way we wanted to play our music," Nelson told Larry King for CNN's *Larry King Live* in 2010. "And

OPPOSITE

Waylon Jennings's wife Jessi
Colter, the main female voice
in the *Wanted! The Outlaws*
album, on a promotional visit
to the famous New Orleans
record store Peaches;
March 8, 1976.

that's really where the term *outlaw*, I think, came into it. . . . You go in there with a small budget, nobody gets to cut up a lot of money. If you go in with a million-dollar budget, then everybody makes a little, but the music may not be that great." Lundvall had signed a contract giving Willie full creative control, so the album had to be released, and it finally hit the stores and airwaves in May 1975.

Unlike Nelson's previous album, *Red Headed Stranger* was an immediate hit. Country and rock fans fell for the new sound of free, uncluttered Spanish guitar and Nelson's dusty and authentic vocals. The record went to #1 on the *Billboard* country chart and the first single, Nelson's cover of Fred Rose's 1940s weepy "Blue Eyes Crying in the Rain, " also hit the spot and went on to win a Grammy award for Best Male Country Vocal Performance. Within a year the album had sold half a million copies, a vast amount in 1970s country music. Critics hailed it as Nelson's long-awaited masterpiece.

Paul Nelson, in *Rolling Stone* in August 1975, compared the record to Bob Dylan's *Pat Garrett and Billy the Kid* and wrote, "I can't remember when a record has taken such a hold on me." *Billboard* was impressed but confused, stating: "This might be called a concept album, or even a message album. Frankly, we haven't figured it out yet." Looking back on the album in 1977, Chet Flippo wrote in *Rolling Stone*, "When this album came out I compared it—favorably—to the Bible. Nelson surpassed himself with this masterpiece." An archetypal "outlaw country" album, *Red Headed Stranger* was the antithesis of the recent "pop country" movement that had taken over the airwaves of country radio.

OUTLAW COUNTRY

After the syrup of the late 1960s Nashville Sound and the effervescent ditties of early '70s pop country, the music was ready to go back to basics and rediscover its roots. The pop country of Anne Murray, Kenny Rogers, John Denver, and even Olivia Newton-John was highly successful commercially, if not artistically. But many Nashville artists, some major names among them, were concerned that country music was being diluted to a degree where there might not be any real country left, on radio at least. In 1974, in response to Newton-John winning

the 1974 CMA Female Vocalist of the Year, a group of country stars met at the Franklin Road home of George Jones and Tammy Wynette and formed ACE, the Association of Country Entertainers, to fight back against country pop. The following year, the reigning CMA Entertainer of the Year, Charlie Rich, when presenting the award to the 1975 recipient, John Denver, set fire to the envelope live on TV for the whole country music world to see. Whether Rich was protesting against John Denver in particular or, as his son claims on his website, he was just having a drink-fueled moment that he thought would be funny; the action drew national and even international attention to the presence of "outsider" artists like Newton-John and Denver within the Nashville family. Fans, too, were looking for a return to a more earthy, roots-based country music, and the industry was beginning to notice the shift in taste.

Jerry Bradley, son of the legendary Nashville producer Owen Bradley, was head of RCA in 1975 and recognized the value of some of the Jennings and Nelson recordings he had in the vaults. Waylon and Willie were selling increasingly larger numbers of albums, two or three hundred thousand on each release. Bradley foresaw the impact of a marketing campaign using Nelson and Jennings within the "outlaw" theme, and went to work compiling suitable tracks for such a project.

Jennings pushed for his pal Tompall Glaser to be included, and since Jennings's wife, Jessi Colter, was basking in the success of her hit song "I'm Not Lisa," she was included in the package as well. Bradley came up with an old western "wanted" poster design and ensured some rock-and-roll credibility by asking *Rolling Stone*'s Chet Flippo to write some liner notes for the compilation. The album, *Wanted! The Outlaws*, captured a moment in time, made superstars of Waylon and Willie, launched classic songs like "Good Hearted Woman" and "My Heroes Have Always Been Cowboys," and, unbelievably for 1976, sold a million copies in its first week, an unheralded achievement in country music at that time.

Bill Ivey, director of Nashville's Country Music Foundation, told the *Baltimore Sun* in 1991, "It was a movement, and it had a huge impact on Nashville. And the winners were the performers. It took country away from being a producer's music, and gave more control to them."

The outlaw movement grew quickly in Nashville, with artists on the singer-songwriter side like Kris Kristofferson and Tony Joe White, and singers like Merle Haggard, Johnny Paycheck, and David Allan Coe. Coe took the outlaw image to new heights, driving around Nashville in a converted hearse and finding considerable success with his album *Rides Again*, which opened with the single "Waylon, Willie and Me." The maverick spirit fused well with a new wave of young writers from Texas—Guy Clark, Steve Earle, Jerry Jeff Walker, Townes Van Zandt, Michael Martin Murphy, and Steve Fromholz. These Texas writers, often dubbed "cosmic cowboys," took the outlaw spirit of Willie and Waylon and played by their own rules, refusing to follow the Nashville format. Unless they had creative control like Waylon and Willie, they'd stay in Texas and make their music as they saw fit. Nashville, ever dependent on new talent and selling large numbers of records, would have to grant more freedoms or accept that country music would establish alternative centers of creativity and business. It would be an ongoing struggle.

For his next album under his own name, Nelson stuck with the progressive country theme, if not exactly 100 percent outlaw, for *The Sound in Your Mind*. Recorded in Garland, Texas, and released in February 1976, it featured Willie and the usual suspects—sister Bobbie, Paul English, Mickey Raphael, Jody Payne, Bee Spears, plus Rex Ludwick augmenting English on drums. The record made it to the #1 position on the *Billboard* country chart and climbed to #48 on the pop album chart. Later that year, with Willie Nelson riding high, Columbia released an album of gospel tracks he'd recorded for Atlantic back in 1973 with producer Arif Mardin, *The Troublemaker*. The album was another country chart-topper, and included "Uncloudy Day," which hit #4 in the country singles list.

OPPOSITE

Willie on stage at the Circle Star Theatre in San Carlos, California, in 1974. The venue, a unique style of theatre in the round, was demolished after a fire in 1997.

TAKING CARE OF BUSINESS

With Willie now selling millions of albums and his concert fees rising dramatically, life was good for the Nelson family. He bought homes, cars, boats, and land; paid off loans that various friends had accumulated; and generally made life comfortable for himself and those around him.

But Nelson, like so many before him, simply wasn't paying attention to the nuts and bolts of his finances. He was inadvertently building an empire of hangers-on as his entourage grew, and at the same time, bills weren't being paid. When the IRS questioned some of the tax information regarding profits declared for the huge 4th of July Picnics, Nelson started to worry about his personal and business management. As documented in some detail in *Texas Monthly* (May 1991), in the summer of 1977 he discovered that Neil Reshen had not been paying the IRS since taking over as his manager. Nelson subsequently fired him and appointed Reshen's assistant Mark Rothbaum in his place.

In 1979, Nelson and Rothbaum began working with an accounting firm to fix the taxation mess. The first problem, they soon discovered, was that all the financial records from 1975 to 1979, the years when Nelson's earnings exploded, had somehow been destroyed. Despite that, the IRS claimed they were due $2 million for each of those years, and Willie, who spent money as it came in, had

Wanted: The Outlaws

SIDE ONE

My Heroes Have Always Been Cowboys ✳
Honky Tonk Heroes ✳ I'm Looking for Blue Eyes
✳ You Mean to Say ✳ Suspicious Minds

SIDE TWO

Good Hearted Woman ✳ Heaven or Hell
✳ Me and Paul ✳ Yesterday's Wine ✳ T for
Texas ✳ Put Another Log on the Fire

RECORDED

Various dates

RELEASED

January 12, 1976

LABEL

RCA Victor

PRODUCERS

Waylon Jennings ✳ Richie Albright
✳ Chet Atkins ✳ Danny Davis ✳ Ray Kennedy
✳ Tompall Glaser ✳ Willie Nelson ✳ Ray
Pennington ✳ Shel Silverstein

Wanted: The Outlaws, despite being mostly culled from older and previously released material, nevertheless became the first country music album to sell one million copies. It was a classic example of a perfect storm of artist talent, imaging, commercial appeal, and an all-in marketing plan that would start a revolution in Nashville's record business.

By 1976, Waylon and Willie, brothers in arms, were presented by their booking agents as outlaws. It was a term originally used in this context by Tompall Glaser's Hillbilly Central publicist, Hazel Smith. By this time they not only looked like outlaws, but they were indeed outlaws, given the constraints Nashville had placed on them and the way they had fought back. And they were beginning to sell serious numbers of records. So was Waylon's wife, Jessi Colter, fresh from a smash of her own with "I'm Not Lisa." The idea for an outlaw package album hit Columbia main man Jerry Bradley as a guaranteed moneymaker. Bradley got Jennings to agree, but he then wanted good friend Tompall Glaser included. Willie went along, as did Colter. He told Vernell Hackett at the *Billboard* Summit, June 6, 2012, "I loved the title 'outlaw' though I don't think any of us were. It sounded good, and I thought it was a great marketing move."

There wasn't much for the artists to do except rerecord a vocal to some existing recordings, and Bradley added a live audience rack to "Good Hearted Woman." The record featured two songs from Waylon, two from Willie, two by Jessi Colter, and two from Tompall Glaser. Nelson's tracks were "Yesterday's Wine," "Me and Paul," and, most significantly, the barnstorming duets with Waylon on "Heaven or Hell" and the album's #1 hit single, "Good Hearted Woman."

Willie onstage with Trigger
at the Spartan Stadium in
San Jose, California, July 1982.
Trigger, acquired back in 1970,
is already displaying
numerous autographs.

ABOVE

Willie Nelson and Charley
Pride in a gold-record
presentation to President
Jimmy Carter at the White
House Oval Office, on
behalf of the Country Music
Association, May 15, 1979.

nothing like that available. Nelson was advised by the accountants to deal with
the situation with a variety of tax avoidance programs, which he followed into
the 1980s without realizing that the advice was actually misguided. Ultimately,
Willie's financial and legal situation worsened by the year, despite the increasing
success of his albums: a situation he confirmed to Robert Draper in *Texas Monthly*
in May 1991.

Just at the time Willie's financial affairs had begun to unravel in the summer
of 1977, Columbia had released *To Lefty from Willie*, an album of covers dedicated
to country singer Lefty Frizell, using tracks that had been in the vault since 1975.
Then in 1978 came *There'll Be No Teardrops Tonight*, the title taken from a famous
song by Hank Williams included in the set. But it was earlier, in January of that
year, that Willie scored big time again in a studio collaboration with his buddy
Waylon Jennings, *Waylon & Willie*. The album—which included their take on Ed
Bruce's ironic "Mammas, Don't Let Your Babies Grow Up to Be Cowboys"—
stayed at the top of the country charts for ten weeks, and was followed by Willie's
biggest solo effort yet, *Stardust*.

STARDUST

Columbia was excited to see what he had in mind for his next album. Nelson, never one to rest on his laurels, was less interested in more outlaw music than everyone else at Columbia Records. He had been deeply affected by Bing Crosby's death in October 1977, and as his mood turned nostalgic he returned to something he had been contemplating over several years, an album of American popular music standards. It would be his take on classics songs by the likes of Hoagy Carmichael, George and Ira Gershwin, Duke Ellington, and Irving Berlin. The record company was bemused, irritated, and less than enthused, as Nelson told the *Guardian* in May 2015: "Record company executives are the worst at it. . . . They didn't see it, they didn't understand it, and automatically they said it wasn't a good idea. I went ahead and did it anyway, because I had it in my contract that I had creative control—I could record anything I wanted to. They had to back off and take it, and when it wound up a No. 1 record, they all said, 'Well, look what we did!'"

Nelson finally scored the right arranger and producer to make his vision a reality when he found common ground with a neighbor, Booker T. Jones, at his apartment complex in California. He told the *Los Angeles Times*, on August 9, 2014, "I had been wanting to do the album for a long time, but I was waiting until I found somebody who could write the arrangements."

> "I COULD RECORD ANYTHING I WANTED TO. THEY HAD TO BACK OFF AND TAKE IT, AND WHEN IT WOUND UP A NUMBER ONE RECORD, THEY ALL SAID, 'WELL, LOOK WHAT WE DID!'" —WILLIE NELSON

Booker T. had started out with the MGs as the house band at Stax-Volt Records in Memphis in 1962, playing on hits like Carla Thomas's "Gee Whiz" and Rufus Thomas's "Walkin' the Dog," as well as their own instrumental smash, "Green Onions." After his time with the band, Booker T. moved to Los Angeles to work as a producer for A&M Records. Among others, he produced his wife, Priscilla Coolidge, and her sister, Rita Coolidge, who was married to Kris Kristofferson. Willie and Connie's girls Amy and Paula loved to play with Kristofferson and Coolidge's daughter Casey, and the Nelsons had actually leased an apartment

in Malibu to spend more time with them. Booker T. happened to live upstairs from the Nelsons, and naturally the two musicians had plenty in common—and plenty to chat about musically, including Nelson's off-the-wall idea to make an album of standards. Nelson wanted to introduce his new younger fans to the music he'd grown up on and he felt that Booker T. would treat the songs respectfully but in a contemporary manner.

"One of the reasons Willie had come to me for the album," Booker T. told Wonderingsound.com in 2011, "was because of how simply I approach everything. I think he really liked that. We had a lot of space on that record, a lot of time to think about the words and the melody."

Reviews ranged from good to great. In July 1978, *Rolling Stone* raved about the album, stating, "In one sense, *Stardust* is a memory album: 'On the Sunny Side of the Street,' 'Georgia on My Mind' and the rest were songs Nelson grew up playing. . . . You can still hear a hint of polka and the clippety-clop of singing cowboys in the bass line of 'Blue Skies,' and the black-tie-and-champagne bounce of 'Someone to Watch Over Me' has been smoothed to a whiskey (straight up) fox trot. A harmonica does the duty of a horn section, and in between the verses Nelson picks out the melody on his guitar. The notes are as sweet and easy as the smiles of the women eyeing the bandstand over their partners' shoulders."

Billboard noted that Nelson put his "distinctive, soft vocal style to good use interpreting a number of standards as well as country-flavored tunes. All of the material seems well suited to his easygoing style, as Nelson backs himself with guitar and gets help with guitar, drums, keyboards, bass, and harmonica."

Hoagy Carmichael's "Georgia on My Mind," the first single from *Stardust*, went to #1 on the country chart and incredibly to #5 on the pop chart. The album was certified platinum in December 1978. It sat in the Top 200 for almost two years, and went on to sell over 5 million copies. Willie Nelson won a Grammy for Best Country Vocal Performance, Male, for his inspired version of "Georgia on My Mind." Moreover, *Stardust* was recently inducted into the Grammy Hall of Fame class of 2015.

✷ Trigger ✷

"Trigger's like me," Willie told *Texas Monthly* in December 2012. "Old and beat up."

The "Trigger" Willie Nelson refers to is his 47-year-old classical guitar, an instrument that's as much a part of Nelson's sound and persona as his distinctive voice, jazz-tinted country songs, flame red hair, beard, and bandana. Nelson had played several types and brands of guitars through the 1950s and '60s, often Fender Stratocaster and Telecaster electrics, Gibson electrics, and assorted acoustics. Trigger, for those not acquainted with 1940s Hollywood Western stars, was the name of cowboy superstar Roy Rogers's trusted steed—an appropriate name for the beat-up old guitar that Nelson's now been playing 250 nights a year for the last five decades.

Back in 1969, after a show in John T. Floore's Country Store (a historic honky-tonk in Helotes, just outside San Antonio), Nelson placed his Baldwin 800C Electric Classic guitar down, only for a worse-for-the-wear reveler to step on it and smash the guitar. Nelson hoped Shot Jackson, the renowned guitar repairman in Nashville, could fix his instrument. Jackson took a look at the broken guitar in his shop at 416 Broadway and broke the news to Nelson that the guitar was not fixable, suggesting that Willie purchase a new 1969 Martin N-20 classical guitar for the princely sum of $750. Nelson liked the sound of the Martin. He explained why in a *Rolling Stone* video interview special narrated by Woody Harrelson in 2012: "It has the tone that I like. It has a

Django-like tone. Django Reinhardt's my favorite guitar player. Any time I can hit a note that sounds anywhere near what he did, I like it, so that's why I got so hooked on Trigger."

Nelson's Trigger is one of only 277 N-20 Martins made between 1968 and 1970. Nelson's broken Baldwin guitar had a built-in ceramic piezo-electric pickup and came with a Baldwin amplifier, giving him a sound he was happy with for both studio and live work. Nelson asked Jackson to take the pickup from the Baldwin and place it in the new Martin. In 1984, he told *Frets* magazine, "I had it taken out of the Baldwin and put in this one years ago, by Shot Jackson's place in Nashville. I've tried to keep everything exactly the same, and the amplifier is still the same one. They don't make Baldwins any more, you know. Each time I come across a used Baldwin amp, I try to buy it so I can use the parts for replacements on this one. I've got a couple of them."

Leon Russell was the first artist to sign Trigger, and instead of writing on the top of the guitar with a pen, Russell carved his name, a tradition followed by hundreds since—from country legends Roger Miller, Kris Kristofferson, Gene Autry, Johnny Cash, and Waylon Jennings to current stars Jack White and Jamey Johnson.

Opposite: Willie on stage with Trigger during the Outside Lands music festival in San Francisco, August 11, 2013.

4

1982 ✳ 1990

Highwayman

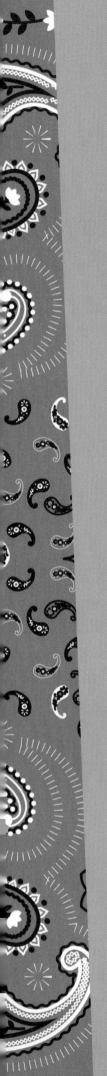

Life for Willie Nelson in the late '70s was everything he had wished for. He was finally established as an artist, not just a songwriter, and he had all the money he could possibly need, enough indeed to bypass the few negatives of fame, like overenthusiastic fans, reporters, and photographers.

He lived in a charming three-level chalet on sixty acres near Denver. There was also his sixty-plus-acre Pedernales Country Club just outside Austin, where he built a recording studio to the design specifications of producer Chips Moman; it was there he recorded the albums *Always on My Mind*, *Tougher Than Leather*, and *Pancho and Lefty*, the latter with Merle Haggard.

"ALWAYS ON MY MIND"

Some albums contain a collection of poor, good, and even great songs, while other records, like Nelson's 1982 offering, *Always on My Mind*, are transcended by one song, one momentous track that lifts the record to another level.

When *Always on My Mind* was released in the spring of 1982, *Rolling Stone* magazine's reviewer Paul Nelson (no relation) was far from impressed, writing, "You haven't lived until you've heard Nelson stumble through Paul Simon's 'Bridge over Troubled Water.' Or how about Procom Harem's classic 'A Whiter Shade of Pale,' in which the star is joined by Waylon Jennings? Doing such material isn't daring, it's dumb. But then, so are most of this album's C&W tunes. What's even worse is that Willie Nelson is now beginning to sound like some unctuous country DJ: he's startlingly insincere, faking emotions instead of feeling them. *Always on My Mind* is strictly paint-by-numbers product."

Producer Chips Moman suggested that Nelson record "Always on My Mind"—written by Wayne Carson, Johnny Christopher, and Mark James—as a duet with Merle Haggard during the *Pancho and Lefty* session, but Haggard was unimpressed with the track. Wayne Carson, an old friend of Merle Haggard, told a Country Music Hall of Fame seminar audience in December 2011: "He leaned back and said, 'Who wrote this piece of shit?' Somebody said, "Wayne Carson." Haggard replied, 'Well, no wonder I don't like it.'"

Nelson however felt he could bring something to the song that had already been recorded by several major artists, including B.J. Thomas, Brenda Lee, and Elvis Presley. It was a song of regret and maybes that came from a guilt-ridden phone call between Wayne Carson and his wife. "I said, 'Well, I know I've been gone a lot, but I've been thinking about you all the time,'" Carson told the *L.A. Times* in 1988. "And it just struck me like someone had hit me with a hammer. I told her real fast I had to hang up because I had to put that into a song."

Producer Chips Moman, who worked in Memphis with Carson, was involved with the song from its early days. Carson completed the number with the help of Johnny Christopher and Mark James, after Moman said the song was missing a bridge.

— WILLIE NELSON ★ AMERICAN ICON —

ABOVE

Willie Nelson and Merle
Haggard (right) remained
close friends until Haggard's
death at age seventy-nine
in April 2016. Here, the two
buddies are performing at
Willie's 4th of July Picnic
in Austin, 2003.

"Always on My Mind" was #1 on the *Billboard* country singles chart for two
weeks and the CMA's 1982 Song of the Year. The album was named Album of
the Year by both the ACM and the CMA. It also won Grammys for Best Male
Country Vocal Performance, Best Country Song, and Song of the Year. The song
is a staple of every Nelson concert, a pin-drop moment, and has become a bona
fide timeless classic. Indeed, in 2007 the British comedy writer and actor Ricky
Gervais chose Nelson's version as one of his must-haves on the long-running
BBC radio show *Desert Island Discs*, explaining: "The Elvis version's beautiful, but
I never considered Elvis vulnerable enough to pull this song off. It's that regret,

it's that guy who's maybe made some mistakes, and now he's in the twilight years and he's trying to put it right. This one, out of all the songs, nearly makes me cry every time."

"PANCHO AND LEFTY"

Nelson had first met Merle Haggard at his house in Nashville in 1964, but the Chips Moman session was their first chance to work together seriously. Haggard, perhaps the ultimate outlaw, avoided day-to-day dealings with the country music establishment by being based in his native California. He was born in 1937 in Bakersfield and raised there by his parents, who had relocated to California from Oklahoma during the Dustbowl crisis of the 1930s. Merle had a troubled youth, and was often involved in petty crime and juvenile delinquency. This escalated in his late teens, and after a failed attempted robbery in 1957, he found himself serving two years and five months in San Quentin Prison. In the penitentiary, he played in a country music band, and after witnessing Johnny Cash's first appearance at San Quentin on New Year's Day 1959, he vowed to make music his career on his release. Along with Buck Owens, Haggard was a pioneer of the "Bakersfield sound," a tough-edged reaction to the slick music coming out of Nashville at the time.

Haggard hit the big time in 1969 with "Okie from Muskogee," a song extolling middle-America conservative values, and although he always claimed the lyrics were deliberately ironic, the tune became a pro–Vietnam War/anti-counterculture anthem. The arch-conservative president Richard Nixon even pardoned Haggard for his crimes in 1972. But Haggard was no reactionary, as the rest of his vast body of work attests. Between the late 1960s and the 1980s, he had no less than thirty-eight country chart-toppers. Despite things slowing down somewhat in the late '70s, he bounced back in 1981 with "Big City," a song that saw him back in top form again as the voice of the worker. It was on the back of this 1980s renaissance that that Haggard and Nelson came up with the idea of a duets album. Nelson, as he preferred to do, ensured that the work element of recording included plenty of play and recreation.

As Patrick Doyle recalled in *Rolling Stone*, "In 1982, they recorded 'Pancho and Lefty' together at Nelson's ranch near Austin, where they'd stay awake for days—'We were living pretty hard in that time period,' Nelson has said—playing golf and then recording all night (Haggard barely remembers singing his famous verse on 'Pancho and Lefty'). At the time, they were fasting on a master-cleanse regimen of cayenne pepper and lemon juice. 'I think Willie went ten days,' says Haggard. 'I went seven.'"

Chips Moman—who had produced Elvis Presley's best tracks in the King's later years, "In the Ghetto" and "Suspicious Minds"—was also an accomplished writer and musician who had known Nelson for some time. As Moman explained

to Georgiarhythm.com: "I loved Willie Nelson when he first came to Nashville. He and I and Roger Miller all signed to Tree Music about the same time. And I was really into a lot of his demos that I was playing on, and hearing up there. I really loved Willie Nelson from the first time I ever heard him."

With Chips Moman at the production desk, Haggard and Nelson raced through almost thirty songs, but even with that many in the can, Nelson felt they were short of that one killer song every top album needs. Lana Nelson, Willie's daughter, had been listening heavily to Emmylou Harris's game-changer 1976 album *Luxury Liner*, and one song in particular, "Pancho and Lefty."

The song had originally been recorded by its writer, Texas musician Townes Van Zandt—one of the singer-songwriter circle of Texas renegades who moved to Nashville in the late '70s—and also included the likes of Steve Earle and Guy Clark. Van Zandt's magnificent Western ballad had first appeared on his 1972 album *The Late Great Townes Van Zandt*, along with another frequently covered original, "If I Needed You."

Willie Nelson fell for the song immediately, and while an exhausted Haggard caught up on his sleep, he started cutting the track. At about four in the morning, Willie woke Haggard to come sing his part. Haggard angrily said no, he'd do it later, but Nelson was insistent, as Haggard recalled to the *Houston Press* in 2013: "He said, 'No, I want you to come in here and sing this motherfucker,' I said, 'OK, goddammit, I will.'"

The beautifully written ballad of a Mexican bandit, Pancho, and his sidekick, Lefty, was a perfect vehicle for Haggard and Nelson, who brought an entirely appropriate world-weariness to the vocals, setting the song off perfectly. As the title track, it was the second single release from Willie and Merle's *Pancho and Lefty* album, and it went to #1 with little effort. Lana Nelson directed the song's accompanying music video and cast Townes Van Zandt in a small a role as one of the Mexican Federales.

The album was a success story for both Nelson and Haggard, ensuring their credibility with the new "cosmic cowboy" crowd, and for the usually broke Van Zandt. *Pancho and Lefty* was up for the Country Music Association's Album of the Year in 1983, but was just edged out by the country rock and bluegrass band Alabama.

FAME AND FORTUNE

Around the same time that the recording studio opened, Willie also purchased an eighty-unit apartment building and the Austin Opry House, a prestigious 1,700-seat theater. Property didn't matter too much to Nelson, except for investment purposes, since he and the Family spent an average of 250 days every year on the road in a highly organized team of three tour buses and two massive trucks for his sound equipment.

Fame and success, of course, couldn't shield Nelson completely from the emotional downs that followed the loss of his father, Ira, on December 5, 1978, from lung cancer, and the death of his grandmother, Mama Nelson, the following November. And in 1983, his mother, Myrtle, would also succumb to lung cancer.

Soothed by his deep belief in reincarnation, Nelson dealt with these losses philosophically, explaining to *Parade* magazine in 2010: "Death is not the ending of anything, I believe all of us are only energy that becomes matter. When the matter goes away, the energy still exists. You can't destroy it. It never dies. It manifests itself somewhere else. We are never alone. Even by ourselves, we are not alone. Death is just a door opening to somewhere else. Someday we'll know what that door opens to."

Willie Nelson came extremely close to death himself in 1981, while swimming in the ocean during a family vacation at a resort in Hawaii. He suffered a collapsed lung and was rushed to the hospital, where doctors treated him by inserting a chest tube to drain the lung. After a few days of rest, his lungs healed themselves. Fortunately no surgery was necessary, but the Texas troubadour was forced to cancel eighteen scheduled concerts, costing him almost a million dollars.

The loss of loved ones and his own flirtation with the infinite left Nelson with a sense of nostalgia for his roots in Texas and a renewed appreciation of the gifts he'd been granted to write songs and perform for millions of adoring fans.

"DEATH IS NOT THE ENDING OF ANYTHING, I BELIEVE ALL OF US ARE ONLY ENERGY THAT BECOMES MATTER. WHEN THE MATTER GOES AWAY, THE ENERGY STILL EXISTS." —WILLIE NELSON

Buoyed by the financial success of his outlaw music and proven right in his belief that an album of nostalgic standards would be a commercial winner, Willie Nelson finished the 1970s with a series of albums that he truly wanted to make. Years of Nashville frustration, of trying to conform, and of rarely being completely happy with the end product found release after the commercial and critical success of *Stardust*. From that point on, he would feel fully satisfied musically. In April 1978, Willie and the Family recorded a bumper two-disc live LP at Lake Tahoe, *Willie and Family Live*. Featuring guest appearances by Emmylou Harris and Johnny Paycheck, the LP topped the country album chart and made the Top 200 pop album chart at #32 on its release in November 1978. The following year he went on to tackle an album of Kris Kristofferson songs, *Sings Kristofferson*, that went on to earn a platinum disc, selling over a million copies in the United States alone. And having enjoyed previously working with Booker T. Jones on *Stardust*, Willie Nelson renewed their

OPPOSITE

Willie poses for a portrait
during the filming of
The Electric Horseman in
Nevada, November 1978.

FOLLOWING PAGES

Willie enjoys a bowl of chili and
cornbread with Texas governor
James T. Thompson, between
his two performances at the
Illinois State Fair, August 1979.

relationship for the 1979 Christmas album *Pretty Paper*, which turned out to be another million-seller.

Willie also rekindled another musical partnership that had begun in the early 1970s, this time with the pianist and vocalist extraordinaire Leon Russell. "Leon came down to the first 4th of July picnic that I had," Nelson told the *L.A. Times* in February 1996, "and it was the first time that the rock 'n' roll crowd had mixed in with the cowboy crowd—the hippies and the rednecks, we were called. So, thanks to Leon, all those wild things started happening." Nelson and Leon Russell toured together in 1979 and worked on what would become one of the finest duet albums of all time, *One for the Road*.

Nelson and Russell eschewed the obvious country and rock-and-roll for the majority of tracks on the double LP and instead recorded older songs and standards, most successfully Cole Porter's "Don't Fence Me In" and Gene Autry's "Ridin' down the Canyon." And the album's first single went to the country #1 spot, a rollicking version of Elvis's "Heartbreak Hotel"—penned of course by Mae Axton, who had encouraged a young Willie Nelson to pursue his musical path many years before.

HOLLYWOOD

It seemed pure serendipity that placed Willie Nelson next to the Hollywood actor and movie producer Robert Redford on a flight from New York to Los Angeles. During their conversation, Redford asked if Willie harbored any desire to try his hand at acting, and when Nelson showed some interest, the movie star suggested that his natural talent as a performer would allow him to take to acting with ease. Redford was working on a movie, *The Electric Horseman*, alongside another Hollywood superstar, Jane Fonda. Redford told Sydney Pollack, the film's much-respected director, that he should cast Willie Nelson in the upcoming movie, and the veteran moviemaker agreed that Nelson could be just the man to play Redford's world-weary manager. Willie breezed through his lines like an old pro, notably the somewhat racy "I don't know about you, but I'm gonna get me a bottle of tequila, find me one of them Keno girls that can suck the chrome off a trailer hitch, and just kind of kick back." Nelson was essentially playing a close approximation of himself in the movie, and when *The Electric Horseman* opened in 1979, he received very positive reviews for his work.

Robert Redford was especially impressed, telling Michael Hall of *Texas Monthly* in 2008, "He's a natural, because he just has an ability to be himself. I don't think you're going to ask him to play King Lear, but that's not what you expect him to do. When they call for somebody to represent a certain kind of texture as a character, he can just slip right into it. He also doesn't put a whole lot of emphasis on it. He's fortunate because it's not his endgame; his music is his endgame. So he can afford to say, 'Yeah, I'll go do this.'"

In his next movie, the 1980 romantic drama *Honeysuckle Rose*, Nelson pretty much played himself again, this time as a maverick country singer whose home life has to compete with his wandering eye and cheating ways on the road. The movie's director, Jerry Schatzberg, told *People* magazine on its release that he was delighted with Willie's performance in front of the camera. "Willie does it like a real person, which is what an actor is supposed to do. He's very natural in the love scenes because he's had a lot of experience there. The man's been married three times and he knows what he's doing."

The *Chicago Sun Tribune*'s esteemed film critic Roger Ebert made special note of Nelson's acting skills when adding up the movie's merits: "It has its charms, and one is certainly the presence of Willie Nelson himself, making his starring debut at the age of 47 and not looking a day over 60. He's grizzled, grinning, sweet-voiced and pleasant, and a very engaging actor."

" IT HAS ITS CHARMS, AND ONE IS CERTAINLY THE PRESENCE OF WILLIE NELSON HIMSELF, MAKING HIS STARRING DEBUT AT THE AGE OF 47 AND NOT LOOKING A DAY OVER 60. HE'S GRIZZLED, GRINNING, SWEET-VOICED AND PLEASANT, AND A VERY ENGAGING ACTOR."

—FILM CRITIC ROGER EBERT ON *HONEYSUCKLE ROSE*

On a plane trip, the executive producer of *Honeysuckle Rose* asked Willie to contribute a tune about life on tour. He quickly scrawled down the lyrics for "On the Road Again," which arguably has been Nelson's trademark song for the past thirty years. His character in the film has a romance with a singer, who is the daughter of a fellow musician. Nelson's real-life chemistry with movie girlfriend Amy Irving (who later married Steven Spielberg) spread into real life and played a major part in Willie and Connie's divorce.

Nelson was featured in a Western movie for his next screen role, *Barbarosa*, alongside a young actor named Gary Busey, fresh from his Oscar-nominated breakout performance in *The Buddy Holly Story*. Then Willie played yet another version of himself in the movie *Songwriter* in 1984, alongside Kris Kristofferson,

OPPOSITE

A still from Willie's 1980 movie *Honeysuckle Rose*, with co-star Amy Irving.

BELOW

The poster for *Honeysuckle Rose*, with Dyan Cannon (left) and Amy Irving as the two loves in the hero's life.

who plays his friend and a fellow country music artist. Nelson's character does not fare well amid the crooks and sharks in the music business, something Nelson could well relate to in real life.

The screenwriter on *Barbarosa* and *Honeysuckle Rose*, Bill Wittliff, liked Nelson's *Red Headed Stranger* enough to put together a movie treatment based on the album. While creating the album, Nelson had imagined the story could be adapted as a movie, as he told *Chicago Sun Tribune*'s Roger Ebert in an interview in November 1986: "When I wrote the album, for some reason I could see a movie being made of it. And I just felt like if it were to be made into a movie, I could probably play that character as well as anybody. I used to sing the song to my kids as a bedtime story."

In the movie Willie plays a preacher who kills his wife and her new lover, and then spends a year on the run before returning to the same town for a final showdown. Nelson persuaded Universal Pictures to option the movie, and the studio attempted to entice Robert Redford into the main role. When that fell through, Nelson slid out of his arrangement with Universal, paid back his advance money, and figured he'd find someone else to make the movie he so dearly wanted to see filmed.

When financing proved almost impossible without a Hollywood name to sell the project, Nelson decided to go it alone—something he had some experience in. He mortgaged his house and built sets on the land next to his recording studio in Pedernales, essentially creating his own western town. Nelson slashed the movie's original budget from $13 million to less than $3 million, cutting the payroll by using local craftsmen and workers, and filling roles in the movie with family, friends, and band members. For the leading roles, both Morgan Fairchild—who played the preacher's cheating wife—and Katharine Ross (the preacher's later love interest) agreed to defer half their fees until the movie made back some money.

For 20 years he's been singing to the country.
But he never figured he'd be living his own love songs.

A SYDNEY POLLACK/GENE TAFT Production A JERRY SCHATZBERG Film
WILLIE NELSON
DYAN CANNON AMY IRVING
HONEYSUCKLE ROSE
Also starring SLIM PICKENS Executive Producer SYDNEY POLLACK
Screenplay by CAROL SOBIESKI and WILLIAM D. WITTLIFF and JOHN BINDER
Based on the story by GOSTA STEVEN and GUSTAV MOLANDER Produced by GENE TAFT
Original songs composed by WILLIE NELSON and performed by WILLIE NELSON and FAMILY
Directed by JERRY SCHATZBERG

Original Soundtrack on CBS Records & Tapes
Read the Bantam Book

From Warner Bros.
A Warner Communications Company [W] [PG] PARENTAL GUIDANCE SUGGESTED
SOME MATERIAL MAY NOT BE SUITABLE FOR CHILDREN
© 1980 Warner Bros. Inc. All Rights Reserved

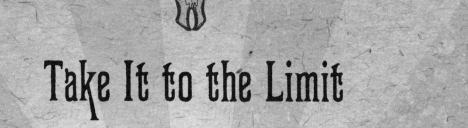

Take It to the Limit

SIDE ONE

No Love at All ✳ Why Do I Have to Choose ✳ Why
Baby Why ✳ We Had It All ✳ Take It to the Limit

SIDE TWO

Homeward Bound ✳ Blackjack County Chain ✳ 'Til
I Gain Control Again ✳ Old Friends ✳ Would
You Lay with Me (In a Field of Stone)

RECORDED

Early 1983

RELEASED

April 1983

LABEL

Columbia

PERSONNEL

Gene Christman, Paul English (drums) ✳ Mike Leach,
Bee Spears (bass) ✳ Willie Nelson, Waylon Jennings,
Chips Moman, Reggie Young, Grady Martin, Johnny
Christopher (guitar) ✳ Bobbie Nelson, Bobby Wood
(keyboard) ✳ Jon Marett (saxophone) ✳ Willie Nelson,
Waylon Jennings, Toni Wine, Lisa Silver, Harry Huffman,
Chips Moman, Bobby Wood, Johnny Christopher,
David Alan Coe, Garry Talley (harmony vocals)

PRODUCER

Chips Moman

Take It to the Limit, released in 1983, again saw Waylon Jennings and Nelson team up for an eclectic mix of country and contemporary covers. This album, unlike the previous Waylon and Willie projects, was released on CBS instead of on Jennings's RCA label, which probably explains the minor change in billing. *Take It to the Limit* features "Willie Nelson with Waylon Jennings," a subtle departure from Willie *and* Waylon.

Nelson shines on Rodney Crowell's "'Til I Gain Control Again" and surprises with a wholly original take on the old Paul Simon nugget and street busker's favorite, "Homeward Bound." The record features mostly Willie and Waylon on separate tracks, but their duet cover of the Eagles' punchy "Take It to the Limit" is worth the price of admission alone. The public hadn't tired of the old outlaw pair, and the album made it as high as #3 in the country charts, with the shimmering title single climbing to #8 in the United States and topping the country best-sellers in Canada.

Reviews at the time were very favorable, with *People* magazine writing: "Anyway, it's just about impossible to keep up with all the permutations Nelson is going through these days, and in this case it really doesn't matter. The album is just full of extraordinary music, whoever is doing it."

Nelson's preacher, who becomes a killer, is a violent man within a violent tale. Nelson told Cheryl McCall of *Life* magazine in August 1987 that he needed that edge to make the movie believable. "If you like the song, the violence is there. You can't take out violence any more than you can take evil out of books. It's all part of life. This movie covers a lot of territory—from spiritualism to lust—and takes a man all the way to the bottom and back to the top. It does it to a preacher—which is a little bit unusual."

The finished movie debuted at the Denver International Film Festival in October 1985 and received a mixed reaction. By cutting corners on personnel, some of the supporting cast lacked the acting gravitas to line up against Hollywood stars like Fairchild and Ross, or even Nelson himself. It gave the movie an uneven timbre, something that unsettled audiences and critics. Texas reviewers were far kinder, understanding perhaps the importance of the movie to Nelson and the homegrown aspect of the production that provided work for so many Texans in the Austin area. The goodwill factor locally was certainly high. Despite some negativity toward *Red Headed Stranger*, Nelson was immensely proud of the movie and was delighted to showcase it at a special press conference in the United Kingdom the following year, where he gladly answered questions after a screening of his pet project.

If *Red Headed Stranger* was a labor of love, then the 1986 remake of the John Ford classic western *Stagecoach* was essentially an opportunity for Nelson and his Highwaymen buddies Cash, Jennings, and Kristofferson to hang out on set and play at "cowboys and Indians" for a few weeks. The CBS made-for-television movie threw a cast of country music friends and legends together, featuring (as well as the four Highwaymen) Cash's wife, June Carter-Cash; John Schneider; Jessi Colter, David Allan Coe; and Billy Swan—and Cash's son John Carter-Cash.

Stagecoach 1986 style was an energetic remake, with Kristofferson excellent as the Ringo Kid, the role that made John Wayne famous in the 1939 original. Nelson plays dentist-meets-gunman Doc Holiday, Waylon plays southern gent and gambler Hatfield, while the heartthrob of the day John Schneider (of *Dukes of Hazzard* fame) plays Buck, the stagecoach driver. The fun factor was recognized by reviewers; *Rolling Stone* magazine, for instance, wrote, "*Stagecoach* cracks its whip by focusing on country star power, not necessarily acting ability."

CHANGING OF THE GUARD

The mid-'80s witnessed another changing of the guard in country music, leaving stalwarts like Waylon and Cash (and Willie, although a little later in his case) struggling to match the record sales of a new young industry, which ironically had been inspired by the back-to-basics outlaw movement of the 1970s.

Indeed, Willie Nelson played a part in the change. His *Electric Horseman* movie opened the eyes of Hollywood to the possibilities in country music, and

the 1980 film *Urban Cowboy*, a massive global hit starring man-of-the-moment
John Travolta, signaled a new wave of pop country, from Eddie Rabbit to T. G.
Sheppard, Sylvia, and Lee Greenwood. Emmylou Harris, the country rock pioneer,
called the new sound "elevator music." Steve Earle, whose breakthrough *Guitar
Town* album in 1986 brought a raw, Waylon-like twang back to country music, told
me in 1992 that country music in the early '80s was so bland it was unlistenable.
"I'd hitchhiked around Texas to see Willie and Waylon, that was real, that was
country music, roots music—but what was on the radio back then was too bland
for a lot of us, who wanted to play a different kind of music."

Country music had become so pop-oriented in the early 1980s that when Kentuckian Dwight Yoakam showed up in Nashville with a vibrant new twist on Buck Owens and Merle Haggard, he was told by the Music City elders that his style was too country! Convinced he was onto something however, Yoakam licked his musical wounds in the punk clubs of Los Angeles before striking a deal with major label Reprise to release the barnstorming *Guitars, Cadillacs, Etc., Etc.* in 1986.

In the meantime, many of the older record company chiefs had passed the torches to younger executives, some of whom sensed a change in the air. New artists like Ricky Skaggs, Alan Jackson, Reba McEntire, and Randy Travis went back to their country roots as a reaction to country pop. They were variously labeled New Country, or New Traditionalists. It was the most significant change in country music since the outlaws in the early 1970s. Country radio, and now television in the shape of CMT (Country Music Television) and TNN (The Nashville Network)—both country versions of MTV—were also helped by a new generation of management and programmers who promoted the new acts to the top of the charts. It was all well and good, but the move left some of the older acts, like George Jones and Tammy Wynette, Dolly Parton, Johnny Cash, Waylon Jennings, and even Willie Nelson, out in the cold. To a degree, Nelson's habit of working in different genres left him less vulnerable to the vagaries of changing trends, but the turnaround finally caught up with him by the middle of the '80s, when his record sales began to flag appreciably.

HIGHWAYMEN

In 1986, Columbia's new Nashville chief Rock Blackburn made the momentous decision to drop Johnny Cash from the label. Around the same time, *Sweet Mother Texas* from February 1986 was Waylon Jennings's final release on RCA Records, which he'd made his artistic home for the previous twenty years. His next album, *Will the Wolf Survive*, was released just a month later on the MCA label. But meanwhile, although Jennings and Cash—and Willie Nelson—may have been under pressure individually, together (with songwriter Kris Kristofferson) they had hit on an unprecedented formula to weather the storm.

The Highwaymen, the ultimate country music supergroup featuring Johnny Cash, Willie Nelson, Waylon Jennings, and Kris Kristofferson, lasted ten years, from 1985 to 1995. They made three albums, two of which went Top 10; had a smash hit single with the first album's title track, "Highwayman" (winning the Best Country Song Grammy award in 1986) and delivered live shows that were momentous in their historic impact and magnificent in their musical power and sheer star quality.

Befitting these troubadour mavericks, the Highwaymen began life accidentally. In 1984, Johnny Cash invited Willie, Waylon, and Kris to come to Montreux, Switzerland, to take part in a TV Christmas special he was shooting there. Inspired by the jam sessions in their hotel rooms after days on the set, when they returned to the United States, the four opted to get back together again when Cash recorded some tracks for his next scheduled album for CBS.

"WITHOUT EVEN THINKING ABOUT IT, I STUMBLED OUT OF BED TO THE PIANO AND STARTED PLAYING 'HIGHWAYMAN.' WITHIN A COUPLE OF HOURS, I HAD THE FIRST VERSE."

—JIMMY WEBB

Looking for suitable material, Cash's guitarist Marty Stuart suggested a Jimmy Webb song that he felt would be perfect for the quartet (who at this time didn't have a collective name). Glen Campbell, who had taken so many Jimmy Webb songs to the top of the charts and had an unreleased version of his own under his belt, dropped by the studio to sing it for the icons. Giving the song a try, the four voices blended like never before.

The song was "Highwayman." Composer Jimmy Webb (whose hits included "By the Time I Get to Phoenix," "Galveston," "Wichita Lineman," and "MacArthur Park") explained to *Performing Songwriter* magazine in 2012 how the Western-themed song came about. "I was in London, finishing an album, *El Mirage*, with George Martin. My friend Harry Nilsson was there, and we were doing some professional drinking. He left my apartment one night, and I went to sleep and had an incredibly vivid dream. I had an old brace of pistols in my belt and I was riding, hell-bent for leather, down these country roads, with sweat pouring off of my body. I was terrified because I was being pursued by police, who were on the verge

of shooting me. It was very real. I sat up in bed, sweating through my pajamas. Without even thinking about it, I stumbled out of bed to the piano and started playing 'Highwayman.' Within a couple of hours, I had the first verse. I don't know how they decided who would take which verse, but having Johnny last was like having God singing your song." The song was the key to the project, allowing as it did the four singers to sing separately but with a common voice.

Nelson's harmonica master, Mickey Raphael, who was on the *Highwayman* album, recalled the special chemistry the four brought to the project when talking to AARP.com in 2016: "Johnny was bigger than life. Kris was the revolutionary, and Willie was the jokester. Waylon was the conscience of the whole thing, very intense, the one who said, 'Don't screw this up.'"

"It just sounded like something where it worked for everybody," Cash told me in a phone conversation in 1988. "I was truly blown away by working with these artists and to have it sound so good was a dream come true. Was there pressure to outperform those legends? No, pressure is working behind a register in the grocery store and praying you make enough money each week to feed your family. What we do isn't pressure, and in the case of Waylon, Willie, and Kris, it was just joy."

Figuring that the "Highwayman" song would be perfect for a multi-artist album, Cash let the track go, even though it was originally planned for his solo offering. Hooking up with producer Chips Moman in Nashville, Jennings, Nelson, Cash, and Kristofferson traded tunes until they had what was felt to be the correct collection of songs to record together. This was outlaw music revisited, but with more folk influence perhaps. It was "Americana" before the phrase was coined, and without the jangly Byrds-style guitars.

There was a camaraderie from the start, as Jennings told Neil Pond of *Music City News*: "We never had any problems. We don't think of each other as superstars. There were no ego trips. We're a lot alike. We've all had our starving days, paid our dues. We have a lot of respect for each other. If you don't record with somebody you like, it ain't gonna be no good."

Kristofferson confirmed the sentiment on NPR's weekend radio show in February 2013: "Every one of these guys was my hero before I even knew them, you know? Because really, the first time I ever heard Waylon, I was a janitor at the recording studio at Columbia Recording in Nashville. And I volunteered to do a Saturday [cleaning shift] when Waylon was doing a demo, and I'd never heard anything like him. It was a real eye-opener to find myself on the same stage with these guys. Because Johnny Cash, as human as he is—or was—he was always larger than life. He always felt like something right off of Mount Rushmore."

The record was officially released in May 1985 as "*Highwayman* by Nelson, Jennings, Cash, Kristofferson" rather than the group name they subsequently used. The title track went to the #1 spot in the country chart, while a second single, Guy Clark's tremendous "Desperadoes Waitin' for a Train" was Top 20. The album itself topped the *Billboard* country chart and made it to a decent #92 in *Billboard*'s Top 200 mainstream pop chart.

In 1990, the band delivered a follow-up, *Highwayman 2*, which was also produced by Chips Moman. A decent enough sequel, if lacking the majesty of the original, the record made Top 10 in the country album charts, but failed to break the Top 10 chart with any of its single releases.

To promote the second album, the Highwaymen went on the road. Their first show as the Highwaymen took place March 3, 1990, at the Livestock Show and Rodeo at the Houston Astrodome, which kicked off a small-scale tour.

If having Nelson, Jennings, Cash, and Kristofferson on TV and in recording studios were exercises in camaraderie, then the live shows that kicked off in Houston were a full-blown fun factory, as Nelson told Kevin O'Hare of the *Republican* on May 12, 2010: "Well we had all our families with us. Most of our

OPPOSITE

Organizers at the first Farm Aid concert in 1985, John Mellencamp (far left), Willie Nelson (second right), and Neil Young (far right), with the Rockmans, two of the farmers assisted by the fundraising event.

wild days were behind us by the time we got together in the Highwaymen. Actually the last two or three times we went on tour, we had all our kids and families, and went to Singapore and Australia and different places. We had 278 pieces of luggage."

The Highwaymen tour made it to Europe in 1992 and included a prestigious sell-out show in April that year at the Wembley Arena in London. The group followed that tour with one more album, the patchy Don Was–produced *The Road Goes on Forever*. Released in 1995, it had the power of the previous albums but no great tunes, and none of the album's singles made any dents in the charts.

"THE LAST TWO OR THREE TIMES WE WENT ON TOUR, WE HAD ALL OUR KIDS AND FAMILIES, AND WENT TO SINGAPORE AND AUSTRALIA AND DIFFERENT PLACES. WE HAD 278 PIECES OF LUGGAGE"

—WILLIE NELSON

FARM AID

Willie, of course, called on his Highwaymen when he put together the lineup of what he hoped would be a benefit concert for America's farmers, Farm Aid. At the historic Live Aid concert in July 1985, a global audience of maybe two billion people watched Bob Dylan, Keith Richards, and Ronnie Wood perform an unmemorable mini-set of Dylan '60s classics. What was remembered, however, were Bob Dylan's comments about the fund-raising mission of the Live Aid project. "I hope that some of the money . . . maybe they can just take a little bit of it, maybe . . . one or two million, maybe . . . and use it, say, to pay the mortgages on some of the farms and, the farmers here, owe to the banks," he growled.

FOLLOWING PAGES

Left to right: Mike Campbell, Willie Nelson, Tom Petty, and Bob Dylan at the inaugural Farm Aid concert, 1985.

The statement baffled and annoyed Live Aid organizer Bob Geldof, who, while understanding the plight of America's farmers as a real problem, didn't see that issue as serious as the immediate death and starvation that he had witnessed

firsthand in Africa. But Dylan's general point resonated with Willie Nelson, a lifelong supporter of America's farmers, and one who knew personally that the problems they faced were serious.

In 2015, *Modern Farmer* magazine noted, "The 1980s were a bleak time for family farmers, especially in America's heartland. A number of factors that included a series of droughts, low crop prices, and high production costs, and bad lending practices, all joined together to strangle the life out of small farms, some of which had been passed down through families over generations." The most serious issue facing the nation's farmers came from the United States Department of Agriculture calling in loans. Many farms were foreclosed on, and the families ordered off the land within 30 days. It was harsh and brutal, and it was widespread, as Nelson told *Family Farmer* in a special column on July 28, 2015: "In the 1980s, as I toured the country on my bus Honeysuckle Rose, I made it a habit to stop in at diners and truck stops, to talk to folks there. I heard familiar stories that brought me back to my upbringing in rural Texas. And it was from those folks that I came to understand the challenges our family farmers and rural residents face . . . and to see what a tremendous resource they are to all of us."

Nelson was concerned and made a few calls. He had a show planned in Illinois and told his booking agent to try to find a venue for a concert to raise money for farmers. He also spoke with the governor of Illinois about the project. He told *Billboard*'s Thom Duffy: "After I talked to Jim Thompson, the governor of Illinois, about doing the first Farm Aid [at the stadium of the University of Illinois], the first thing I did was call Neil [Young] because I knew he felt the same way I did. It was easy to sell these guys on the idea because they go down the road every day like I do, and they talk to all kinds of people every night, farmers and others. And they knew the problem was getting more and more serious. They were the first to say, 'Yes, let me help.'" Nelson's efforts, alongside Neil Young and John Mellencamp, resulted in the very first Farm Aid concert on September 22, 1985, in Champaign, Illinois, in front of some 80,000 music fans. Nelson's contact list went to good use: a host of music superstars showed up to help the cause, including Bob Dylan, Billy Joel, Bonnie Raitt, B. B. King, Loretta Lynn, Roy Orbison, Alabama, Hoyt Axton, the Beach Boys, Bon Jovi, Glen Campbell, the Charlie Daniels Band, John Denver, John Fogerty, Foreigner, Vince Gill, Arlo Guthrie, Sammy Hagar, Merle Haggard, Daryl Hall, Emmylou Harris, Don Henley, Waylon Jennings, Randy Newman, George Jones, Rickie Lee Jones, Carole King, Kris Kristofferson, Huey Lewis, Roger McGuinn, John Mellencamp, Roger Miller, Joni Mitchell, the Nitty Gritty Dirt Band, Tom Petty and the Heartbreakers, Charley Pride, Lou Reed, Kenny Rogers, Brian Setzer, Tanya Tucker, and Joe Ely.

It was one of the most star-filled benefit concert lineups ever assembled. The benefit was successful musically—in fact, it would have been difficult not to be, given the musical pedigrees on show in Champaign. More importantly to the musicians involved and the fans—and to Nelson, Young, and Mellencamp in particular—the event was a significant success for the people it was designed to help, financially and spiritually.

"To All the Girls I've Loved Before"

SIDE A

To All the Girls I've Loved Before

SIDE B

I Don't Want to Wake You

RECORDED

1983

RELEASED

February 1984

LABEL

Columbia

PERSONNEL

Julio Iglesias, Willie Nelson (vocals) ✳ Mike Landau, David Williams (guitar) ✳ Nicky Hopkins (keyboards) ✳ Carlos Vega (drums) ✳ Stan Getz (saxophone) ✳ Luis Conte (percussion)

PRODUCER

Richard Perry

The Spanish-born singer and songwriter Julio Iglesias initially had athletic ambitions. He rose through the ranks of the top soccer team Real Madrid to become the reserve team goalkeeper. But his soccer dreams were dashed in 1962, when a car accident almost ended his life. In 1968, Iglesias entered a singing contest and won it with a song he wrote himself. That success won him a recording contract in Spain with Discos Columbia (the Spanish arm of Columbia Records), and he subsequently sold millions of singles in Europe, in both Spanish and Italian. In 1979, Iglesias moved to Miami and signed with sister company Columbia International. His first English-language hit was the worldwide smash "Begin the Beguine" in 1983, taken from his million-selling *De Niña a Mujer* album.

Willie Nelson inquired as to whether Iglesias would be interested in a duet. After receiving a positive response, he invited the Spanish singer down to the ranch in Austin for some studio time. The result was the overtly slushy and romantic "To All the Girls I've Loved Before," released in February 1984, which launched Iglesias in the United States. As Iglesias told CNN's *Talk Oasis* in 2014, "The whole thing—you know, it was such an unusual duet that the people reacted wonderfully. And also Willie, he's a natural. He's an incredible guy."

Nelson scored his biggest global hit so far with the single, and later the same year he and Iglesias were voted Duo of the Year by the Country Music Association. And CMA's rival industry organization, the Academy of Country Music (ACM), honored "To All the Girls I've Loved Before" as single of the year.

Rhonda Perry, from the Missouri Rural Crisis Center and Patchwork Family Farms, told *Time* magazine in 2010, "The concert was one of those moments where farmers walked in and had . . . this feeling of elation and you just almost wanted to cry. It made us at least know that people are watching."

Farm Aid was no one-off benefit gesture by Nelson, Young, and Mellencamp. Nelson kept up the annual concerts, and in the 1990s moved the attention to issues involving the growth of factory farming and the issue of small farmers losing out to the pollution of the environment from factories. But Farm Aid, with Nelson at the helm, has never lost sight of its mission of providing practical help to the nation's farmers, and the concerts have been consistently successful at raising both awareness and dollars. As stated on the Farm Aid website at the end of 2016: "Farm Aid has raised more than $50 million to promote a strong and resilient family farm system of agriculture."

BELOW

Willie Nelson performing on stage in 1986, by the famous music photographer David Redfern.

5

1990 ✶ 1998

Who'll Buy My Memories?

Willie Nelson was always the wandering troubadour. He had truly loved all his wives, but the touring lifestyle and his affection for late-night drinking, smoking, and assorted revelries caused problems with every marriage.

Nelson and his third wife, Connie, finally split in the early 1980s, and he was hardly looking for wife number four when he filmed *Stagecoach* with his Highwaymen pals Johnny Cash, Waylon Jennings, and Kris Kristofferson.

ANNIE

Willie's makeup artist for the movie, Annie D'Angelo, first got Nelson's attention when, contrary to direction, she advised him to refuse to let anyone cut his hair for the movie role. Nelson agreed with her, and a bond was born, a bond that grew into romance—and eventually marriage, on September 16, 1991, at St. Alouin Church in Nashville. Annie was spiritual, worldly, intuitive, and independent, as good a match for Nelson as anyone could imagine.

"I'm not easy to live with. I'm pretty temperamental, you know. I've been used to doing things my own way for so long that I'm not interested in any suggestions. There was friction with my other wives. But it seems like Annie and I did okay with each other. It takes a special person to live with me," he told Parade.com in 2010.

Nelson and D'Angelo got together just before the country superstar faced potential financial ruin, but their partnership and eventual marriage was strong enough to cope. Looking back on his final marriage in 2015, Nelson told *Rolling Stone* magazine's Patrick Doyle, "She's been with me through thick and thin—you can't ask for anything more than that!"

Nelson and Annie's two children, Lukas Autry and Jacob Micah, were born in 1988 and 1990, respectively, before Willie and Annie wed. Nelson, perhaps determined to get things right as a parent with his latest family unit, decided to move his wife and kids back home to Abbott, Texas.

Nelson's nostalgia for the rustic, simple upbringing he'd enjoyed in the 1930s was not, of course, possible for his own children. Willie's childhood was simple and frugal, and while much had stayed the same in Abbott, this time around Nelson was a superstar.

Nelson might have wanted to live the simple life, but others—fans, photographers, and reporters—made it unfeasible. Once fans found out he was living back in small-town Texas, a normal family life became impossible. The experiment ended one night when a drunken fan, looking to meet with Willie, drove his truck right into the family home. Willie grabbed Annie and the kids, and they left that night, back to Austin and to the safety of a more secure situation.

Nelson's notion of raising his and Annie's children with good old-fashioned small-town values did seem to have worked however, as Lukas Nelson told the *Humboldt Beacon* in 2011. He said he "was never spoiled when I was a kid. There was never a social separation status-wise between me and any other kids. I always hung out with whoever. Some friends had money and some didn't—it didn't matter. It still doesn't. My parents were against all that because they grew up from humble beginnings."

In fact Lukas and Jacob did have more humble beginnings than their siblings from Willie's previous marriages, since they were both infants when Nelson's financial world came crashing down around him and his family. In November 1990, the federal government raided Willie Nelson's home near Austin. The raid and seizure wasn't a complete surprise to Nelson, but it was most definitely a shock when it actually occurred.

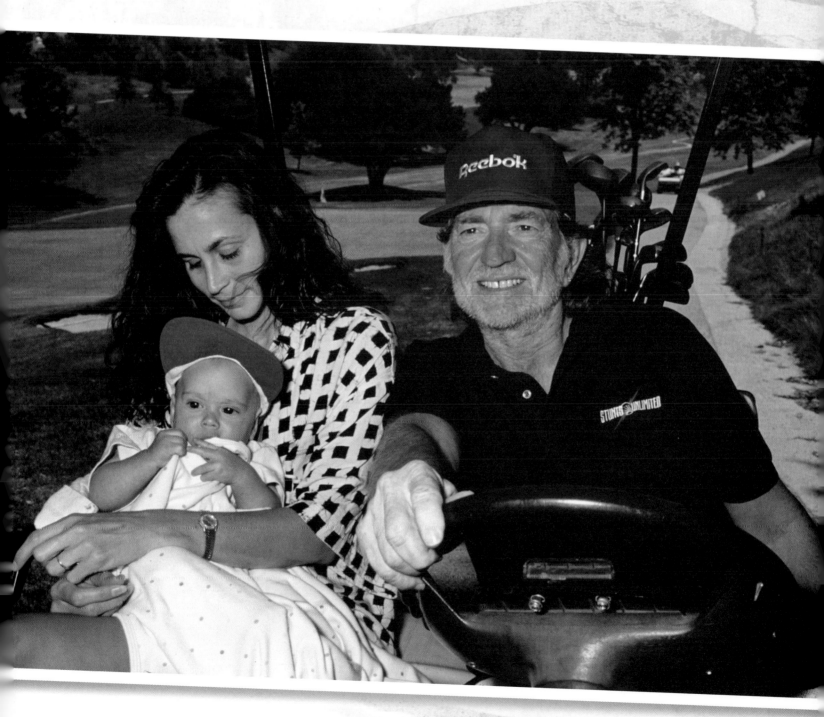

MELT DOWN

As he explained to CNN's Larry King in April 2010, the roots of the raid went back to the 1980s: "Well, I had invested in some tax shelters for many, many years ago, you know, the cattle-feeding things, and all those different things that at some point the IRS disallowed. . . . So, I was deferring taxes every year and putting them into the cattle-feeding deal, and when they disallowed it that meant all those years went by that I hadn't paid taxes. It started out I only owed $2 million. If I paid them that, I would have never had a problem. Penalties and interest every day went up like $5,000 or $10,000. So, it really got up to $32 million, and then they chopped it down in half, and then we negotiated on that."

The tax shelter was indeed a significant part of Nelson's taxation problem. The IRS had begun investigating Nelson back in the 1970s, when the overly modest earnings reported failed to match the presumed (and far more likely) income from million-selling albums and successful concert tours.

Nelson owed the IRS an accumulated sum of some $32 million by the spring of 1990. His attorney managed to skillfully negotiate that figure down to $16 million,

which broke down to $6 million in taxes and $9 million in interest and penalties. The least the IRS wanted to see was a payment of $2 million by September 1990.

Nelson chose not to pursue bankruptcy as an option, and instead set about finding money to satisfy the IRS. But it was a serious problem. Willie had never been one to put money away for his future, and by 1990 his earnings were down significantly compared to his commercial heyday of the 1980s. Daughter Lana told *Texas Monthly* in May 1991, "He had more expenses going out than he had concerts coming in. We've been living hand-to-mouth for the last couple of years."

The country music landscape had altered significantly by the mid-1980s, after the changing of the guard at the beginning of the decade (see pages 123–24). Older acts like Merle Haggard, Hank Williams Jr., Loretta Lynn, and other '60s stars still sold records, but the young new acts that had recently burst on the scene were getting all the attention—and most of the radio play and record sales, with an increasingly young audience. George Strait, alongside younger artists like the Judds and Dwight Yoakam, were taking country music in a hip new direction, a direction that would find its commercial peak when Garth Brooks revolutionized county music marketing and sales when he surfaced in 1989.

Nelson's commercial career was on a downward curve, as reported in detail in *Texas Monthly* in May 1991: he brought in over $14 million on the road in 1985, but that had dropped to just under $5 million in 1989. That was income, not profit, and Nelson's tours were vast and expensive. Record sales had also dipped to a still-decent $300,000 income per album, but with an entourage and a team of family and workers to feed and house, that was small change. Nelson also owed CBS Records several million dollars in recording contract advance payments. Somewhat cavalier with selling his material in his early days, in August 1990 he sold Willie Nelson Music, his song publishing company. But after paying bank loans and numerous debts, Nelson was left with a pittance from the sale, around $35,000. So, despite his good intentions, Willie failed to find the required $2 million to keep the Internal Revenue Service off his back. It was then, on November 9, 1990, that the IRS opted to seize his properties and belongings.

The agents for the IRS took everything they could (although, fortunately, Willie had already instructed his daughter Lana to get his beloved guitar Trigger out of the house and into hiding)—Pedernales Country Club, his ranch, his twenty-odd properties located in several states, his instruments, sound equipment, buses, recording materials, tapes, and all his career memorabilia.

Fans, devastated at the thought of Nelson losing everything, began fundraising efforts in Texas and beyond. Some groups bought Nelson's belongings back from the IRS to return to their hero, and then started a number of charity drives to help pay the singer's tax bills. One group, the Willie Nelson and Friends Showcase, negotiated with a sympathetic IRS agent to buy back memorabilia, guitars, gold and platinum records, and other personal items, for a meager $7,000. The items were then given back to a touched and grateful Willie Nelson.

An Austin club owner, James White, started a "Where There's a Willie, There's a Way" fund, with bands and singers putting on a "Willie Weekend"

BELOW

Austin club owner James White, who helped raise funds towards Willie's tax bill with a "Willie Weekend" benefit show.

benefit show at his Broken Spoke nightclub. And old friend Merle Haggard contacted Nelson, offering to record another duets album, with all the profits going to Willie.

On November 30, 1990, Nelson, calling by phone from his home in Hawaii, told *Entertainment Weekly* magazine: "It's really nice that they want to do something. This whole thing is damn near forcing me to declare bankruptcy. . . . I didn't want to take the chance of getting everybody in the band together and booking a tour, and then finding those IRS guys in our face every night. We're safe here for a while, unless the leaseholders call in the debt I'm starting all over again. It's kind of liberating—just me and my acoustic guitar."

THE IRS TAPES

The plan was to put together a cheaply produced album, using the profits to pay back the IRS. But with the government now owning his music library—including demo tapes, rough song ideas, and almost finished tracks from his studio in Austin—Nelson's usual source of material for a new record was unavailable at the time.

With necessity as the mother of invention, Nelson quite brilliantly chose to rerecord some of his best-known songs himself with just his guitar, Trigger. Nelson selected the songs that he felt would suit the concept and the situation the best, such as "Yesterday's Wine," "Remember the Good Times," and "Wake Me When It's Over."

"It's no overproduced album with millions of dollars of studio costs," Nelson told the *New York Times* in September 1991. "But I think it's the best stuff I got. I've always wanted to put out an album with me and my guitar doing my original songs. And my fans like it because it sounds like it's just me in my living room singing."

"THERE ARE MORE SERIOUS PROBLEMS IN LIFE THAN FINANCIAL ONES, AND I'VE HAD A LOT OF THOSE."

—WILLIE NELSON

The IRS Tapes: Who'll Buy My Memories? was priced at $19.95. As outlined at Forbes.com in April 2013, of that, $9.95 per sale was paid to the record's TV marketing company, $2.40 to Nelson's record company, $2 (significantly, given the circumstances) for future tax bills, $1 for a legal fund, $1.60 for production costs, and $3 to the IRS for back payments, interest, and penalties, as negotiated with the Austin office. The lawsuit brought against the accountants was eventually successful, and Nelson was able to cover the rest of his tax bills and move on.

Willie and Annie, focusing on their two small children, worked hard at keeping the financial crisis in perspective. "There are more serious problems in life than financial ones, and I've had a lot of those," Nelson told the *New York Times* in 1991. "I've been broke before and will be again. Heart broke? That's serious. Lose a few bucks? That's not."

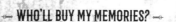

HEARTBREAK

Ironically, while Nelson and his family were heavily embroiled in regrouping after the IRS trauma, a heartbreak of the worst kind happened. On December 26, 1991, the day after Christmas, Willie's son Billy committed suicide. The *Associated Press* reported: "Billy Nelson, the son of country singer Willie Nelson, hanged himself with a cord in his home, authorities said. He was 33. A friend found the body Wednesday, and Medical Examiner Dr. Charles Harlan ruled the death a suicide. Willie Nelson was in Abbott, Texas, when told of his son's death, police said. A Nelson spokeswoman, Evelyn Shriver, reported that Nelson was 'very sad and trying to deal with it.'"

Billy, the son of Willie and Martha, had struggled for some time to make his mark in the world. Dissatisfied with where he fit in, Billy turned to alcohol, which then became an addiction. Billy Nelson had been undergoing rehab for alcoholism in 1990 and was seemingly doing better by the end of the following year.

Nelson's management issued a statement explaining that Willie and his son Billy had spent some time together in the weeks before Billy hanged himself. "Willie was here in Nashville the week before last and spent some time with Billy, and everyone thought everything was fine. Willie's a firm believer in reincarnation and all of that, you know, so that makes it easier to take."

Before his depression-induced death, Billy had been working on recording a gospel album in his own right, with Willie helping out on vocals. The project had kicked off in 1987, but was derailed when Nelson Sr.'s tax problem surfaced; as the government seized most of Willie's tapes and recordings, it took a while for the gospel recordings to be located. Working with the local IRS office in Austin, Nelson negotiated hard to have the government release back to him the thirty-plus years of tapes that had been on the shelves of his recording studio.

Once the tapes were returned, Nelson picked up the project he had worked on with his son and determined to finish the album. The release was marketed via TV, and the label put together a video tribute to Billy for the album's first single, focusing on Willie Jr. recording a rendition of "My Body's Just a Suitcase for My Soul" in the studio.

BRANSON

Despite the trials and tribulations, Nelson was still trying to find a workable balance in his life for his new young family. Moving back to Abbott with Annie and his young kids hadn't worked out, so his next plan—in order to provide some stability, and skip some of the incessant traveling that he believed had damaged his previous marriages—was to stay put for six months in Branson, Missouri, the budding home of country music theater concerts.

Branson, a small town in the beautiful Ozark mountains, had become a mecca for country fans since 1983, when the former star of the *Hee Haw* country TV show, guitar picker Roy Clark, opened a full-time theater. It was essentially Las Vegas for country music fans. Fans went to Branson for a country music vacation, stayed in town for a weekend or more, and helped establish a thriving tourist industry for the area. The 1960s star Mel Tillis opened a theater and made millions of dollars in a short period.

Likewise, Andy Williams opened a theater, and Glen Campbell opened the Glen Campbell Goodtime Theatre in 1994. Waylon Jennings, Johnny Cash, Dolly Parton, Mickey Gilley, Boxcar Willie, Ray Stevens, and Moe Bandy all played long-term dates in Branson. It was a natural home for older country stars and their typically older fans, who didn't especially care for the "New Country" sounds featured on radio and television in the late 1980s and early 1990s.

In 1991, the TV news show *60 Minutes* called Branson the "live music capital of the entire universe." Branson was ideal for artists; the band and family could stay in one place, the kids could enjoy the safe whimsy and charm of the town, and fans would come to them rather than artists traveling to different cities to play for their adoring hordes. When Mel Tillis wanted a break and offered a six-month theater lease to Nelson, the veteran entertainer was interested and pulled in Merle Haggard to work the project with him.

Nelson wasn't as well suited to Branson as he had hoped, however. The town was picturesque but small, and it had yet to build the roads and facilities necessary for the number of tourists that flooded in to see the all-star entertainment. Hotel life didn't suit Nelson either; he felt trapped and restricted by the monotony of sameness—same hotel room, same stage, same faces, same thing every day. To make things work, Nelson and his band were forced by simple economics to play for half their usual fees. And unlike regular touring, they were contracted to play two sets a day, five days a week. On top of that, Willie was expected to find time for after-show fan meet-and-greet sessions, where he and the band would spend an hour or two signing autographs after every concert.

Many Branson tourists had booked tickets to shows years in advance. When Nelson and Haggard suddenly advertised their shows, fans were already committed to alternative attractions. The pair, remarkably, often played to half-full auditoriums attended by dozing elderly country music fans.

Merle Haggard recalled the less-than-satisfying experience on Montereycountyweekly.com in February 2008: "A guy like Willie and I, we thought we could go down there and kill 'em. Well, we went down there and killed 'em all right. Ha. Learned a good lesson. It was the most horrible thing I ever did in my life. We played two shows a day, and we spent three hours going to work and three hours coming home. And we only lived a mile and a half away."

NEW COUNTRY

With over thirty years in the recording industry under his belt, Willie Nelson understood all too well the vicissitudes to be expected in the music industry. Artists typically come and go, and genres enjoy peaks and valleys of mainstream popularity. Country music had enjoyed highs and lows in regard to its popularity, quality, and impact on the mainstream music scene. Sometimes change appears slowly and steadily; at other times it feels more like a radical shift, a revolution that shakes the traditional world to its core. That was what happened to the country music industry before and after the Garth Brooks phenomenon.

It wasn't so much the stylistic change that occurred in the late '80s and early '90s that affected Willie Nelson. He'd never been a flavor of the month artist in the first place. It was more to do with the scale of the enterprise. Country music record sales increased by a staggering 50 percent in 1990, and jumped again the following year when the country music business hit the $1 billion sales mark for the first time in its long history. The globally

popular and genre-busting Garth Brooks was outselling not just country acts but rock, pop, and dance acts as well. In his wake, new artists were breaking through and immediately selling massive numbers of records. Nashville had never seen anything like it. In 1993, total sales added up to nearly $2 billion, with numerous country artists being awarded gold discs (for 500,000 copies sold) for an album. Much of the change was down to the relatively new medium of music video. By the late 1980s, country music had two fulltime music TV channels, CMT (Country Music Television) which was Nashville's version of the MTV phenomenon, and the more talk-oriented and traditional TNN (The Nashville Network).

For established acts like Willie Nelson, Dolly Parton, and Merle Haggard—country music royalty, in effect—the sheer number of new acts who were scoring airplay and mega sales was a real threat. Record industry executives, becoming used to seeing albums sell a half a million or a million (platinum awarded) copies, were less enthused by the solid-selling releases from the likes of Nelson, which sold maybe a quarter of that.

ACROSS THE BORDERLINE

They were decent numbers in the past, but with country enjoying a boom, to typically near-sighted records chiefs, Nelson became a target. Indeed, according to his autobiography, in 1993 he was let go by his record company, in the same year he'd released the progressive and wonderfully received *Across the Borderline* album. The timing on the part of the record company was strange indeed, as the album crossed several genres and was partly recorded in Dublin, Ireland. It picked up favorable attention from both rock and country media.

Across the Borderline was produced by pop-and-rock hit maker Don Was (fresh from glowing reviews for his work with Bonnie Raitt and the B-52s), and saw Nelson tackling songs by ace writers like Ry Cooder, John Hiatt, and Lyle Lovett, and teaming up with a slew of pop and rock artists. He dueted with Paul Simon on Simon's composition "American Tune," delivered his own pleasantly meandering version of Simon's pop classic "Graceland," and sang Peter Gabriel's "Don't Give Up" with Sinead O'Connor and "Getting Over You" with blues-rock luminary Bonnie Raitt. Nelson also co-wrote and recorded a new song with Bob Dylan, "Heartland." Dylan and Nelson, while never great friends, had a long and lasting mutual respect for each other as artists and writers. It was Kris Kristofferson who connected the two in 1972, when he invited Nelson to visit the set of Sam Peckinpah's *Pat Garrett and Billy the Kid* movie in Mexico, in which he and Dylan were cast as Billy the Kid and the enigmatic Alias, respectively. After shooting was over one afternoon, Nelson played some songs, and Dylan was more than impressed. Kristofferson told *Billboard* in 2013 that "Bob Dylan was so knocked out that he made him keep playing. Dylan was just amazed."

Nelson also contributed some originals from his own hand: the lilting ballad "Valentine"; "She's Not for You," which he had written over thirty years before and had kept on the shelf; and the whimsical "Still Is Still Moving to Me."

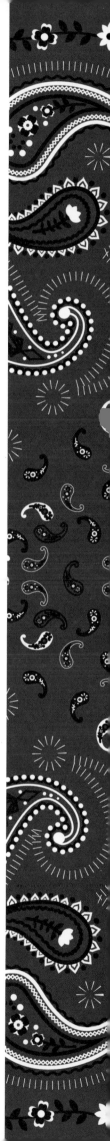

Don Was found it fascinating to work with Nelson, admiring his unique way of working in the studio. As he told the *Detroit Free Press*, "The title song was recorded in Dublin, live in the studio in one take! After we finished tracking the song, we asked the engineer to mix it for us right away. A mix can take a while and Willie had no desire to sit around the studio all day. So he rolled a spliff, and informed the engineer that the mix would be considered finished when the joint was smoked three-fourths of the way down. Sure enough, we had a completed record 20 minutes later. It's the best track on the album!"

Critic Rick Mitchell of the *Houston Chronicle* lauded Nelson's return to classic "Stardust" form, writing that the album was "obviously an important album for Willie Nelson. But it's also an important album for American music. If any artist can surmount the artificial boundary separating country and pop, it's Nelson. He's done it before, and he just might do it again."

Entertainment Weekly was similarly impressed, noting: "Overshadowed in recent years by Garth-mania, Nelson has now topped Brooks in the creation of an album that cuts across the borderline of country into every precinct of pop. As the artistic refinancing of a nearly bankrupt career, this album could have been called Paid in Full." The public agreed and bought the album into the pop charts, the first time a Willie Nelson solo album had managed that since 1985.

"AS THE ARTISTIC REFINANCING OF A NEARLY BANKRUPT CAREER, THIS ALBUM COULD HAVE BEEN CALLED PAID IN FULL"

—*ENTERTAINMENT WEEKLY* ON *ACROSS THE BORDERLINE*

In June 1993, Ireland's top rock publication, *Hot Press*, was more than impressed with the release: "The album's centre-piece is the mellow, and again elegiac 'Across the Borderline,' which was written by Ry Cooder and recorded in Dublin's Windmill Lane Studio. Kris Kristofferson provides backing vocals and the breath-sensitive musical accompaniment comes courtesy of some of Nashville's finest session men—Mike Leech, Robbie Turner, and Reggie Young. To hell with why this album came into existence; it contains Will Nelson's best work in nearly twenty years."

Despite reaching #75 in the *Billboard* Top 200 mainstream chart, the record would be Nelson's last with Sony records for some time. Nelson's contract was up, and he wrote in his autobiography that he felt that even though his sales were reasonable, the company opted for newer and younger acts. Nelson's manager was furious at Sony for dropping a legend like Nelson, as they had with Cash just a handful of years previously. Cash had enjoyed a revival in popularity in the wake of the snub, but he could never see past the insult. Nelson was more philosophical. He had, after all, been fighting with executives since the 1950s. Nothing could really surprise him at this point, and besides there were other record labels, independent or otherwise, where he could surely hang his hat.

HALL OF FAME

Just as the veteran performer and his label were parting ways, the industry, under the aegis of the Country Music Association, bestowed one of its most prestigious honors upon Willie. He was voted by members of the CMA to be inducted into the Country Music Hall of Fame during the 1993 Country Music Association Awards.

On September 29, at Nashville's Opry House, the country music industry's male leadership donned black tie and cowboy boots, and their women companions wore their hair proud and high, while Nashville's new stars graced the stage.

Vince Gill won five awards, including entertainer, male vocalist, album (*I Still Believe in You*), and song of the year ("I Still Believe in You"). Alan Jackson won two CMAs for music video and single of the year via his upbeat hit "Chattahoochee," and Mary Chapin Carpenter was named female vocalist of the year. Mark Chesnutt, Diamond Rio, and Brooks & Dunn were also winners from the new act contingent. It was a star-studded spectacle for sure, but the audience saved its true awe and respect for the moment a raspy-voiced Johnny Cash walked on stage—giving the proceedings a measure of much needed gravitas and solemnity—and proceeded to speak reverentially about his old friend Willie Nelson, as he inducted the Abbott, Texas, boy-made-good into the Country Music Hall of Fame.

Nelson was visibly touched and humbled by the tributes from Cash and then Kris Kristofferson. Swapping his usual jeans and bandana for full tuxedo attire, Nelson explained his more formal look by announcing to the audience, "I really thought you had to die to get here. So I went ahead and dressed up just in case."

CAMPAIGNER

Nelson was of the opinion that maybe his long-term history of outspoken support for various groups, including America's farmers, as well as his pot-smoking reputation, might have made him a target for the government. But those suspicions didn't stop him campaigning on a pro-cannabis and pro-hemp platform in the early '90s with the radical Kentucky politician Gatewood Galbraith. Galbraith wore a hemp suit and traveled the country with Nelson in the "Hempmobile," a car converted to run on hempseed oil. "He's smart and funny and he speaks the truth," Nelson said of Galbraith. "He's a champion for the farmers, and the working men and women of the world."

Government target or not, Nelson was arrested in 1994 after pot was found in his possession as he slept in his car. At 9:00 a.m. on May 10, a police officer investigated a car that he saw parked near the highway. The officer discovered a man asleep in the back seat, a marijuana cigarette in his hand. Nelson had been playing a poker all-nighter and was driving home along Interstate 35 near Waco, Texas, when he decided to stop for a nap and pulled off the highway. The officer told the Associated Press at the time, "We found less than two ounces of marijuana in the car, it was in both a bag and rolled cigarettes." The charges were quashed six months later when Nelson appeared in court (missing the Grammy awards in the process) and witnessed the judge rule the search of his car illegal. In September 1998, Nelson told *Entertainment Weekly*, "There was no cause to give me any problems there that night, because I wasn't botherin' nobody. When it's foggy and you're tired, you pull over and go to sleep. You shouldn't be harassed by the police department."

ISLAND

After the move from Sony, Nelson released *Moonlight Becomes You*, a *Stardust*-style album of old pop standards on the Texas indie label Justice, followed by *Healing Hands of Time*, a 1994 collection of standards that came out on Liberty/EMI. The records were standard Nelson fare—decent, musical, and loved by the fans—but the industry sensed that Willie was treading water. He was releasing too many albums that were just "okay." Perhaps preoccupied with getting his finances back on track, Willie was missing that gem of artistic inspiration and authenticity that had made him a bona fide game-changing artist over the past four decades.

That was soon to change when Nelson recorded his next project, *Spirit*, with just his sister Bobbie on keyboards, fiddle maestro Johnny Gimble, and a second guitarist, Jody Payne. The recordings were an intimate exercise in simplicity, and Nelson went looking for the right record company.

Nelson explained the scenario to Melinda Newman of *Billboard* in April 1996, prior to the album's June release: "Here I was between labels, looking for someone to put out the *Spirit* album which I had already produced myself. In the

BELOW

Willie as Johnny Dean in the acclaimed 1997 comedy film *Wag the Dog*, starring Robert De Niro and Dustin Hoffman.

Spirit

TRACK LISTING

Matador ✳ She Is Gone ✳ Your Memory Won't Die in My Grave ✳ I'm Not Trying to Forget You ✳ Too Sick to Pray ✳ Mariachi ✳ I'm Waiting Forever ✳ We Don't Run ✳ I Guess I've Come to Live Here in Your Eyes ✳ It's a Dream Come True ✳ I Thought About You, Lord ✳ Spirit of E9 ✳ Matador

RECORDED

Spring 1996

RELEASED

June 1996

LABEL

Island

PERSONNEL

Willie Nelson (lead guitar, vocals) ✳ Bobbie Nelson (piano ✳ Johnny Gimble (fiddle) ✳ Jody Payne (rhythm guitar, backing vocals)

PRODUCER

Willie Nelson

If a host of rock-and-roll luminaries could issue striped down, back-to-basics albums in the 1990s, inspired by the incredible success of MTV's acoustic-oriented *Unplugged* series, then Nelson could surely maximize the potential of a less-is-more recording. *Spirit* simply features Nelson on his guitar, Trigger, Bobbie on piano, and the legendary Johnny Gimble on fiddle. It's sparse and wonderfully melodic, and the sibling understanding that Bobbie and Willie Nelson share gives all the tracks an effortless simplicity that's both charming and compelling.

Critics like Chris Morriss at Trunkworthy.com likened the project to Johnny Cash's momentous 1994 comeback album. "*Spirit* has certain similarities to the much admired *American Recordings* album that Johnny Cash worked on with super cool producer Rick Rubin, but Nelson didn't need anyone else to reframe his sound or his position in popular music. Nelson, as he had done several times in the past drew on his own musical roots, looked back to look forward and recognized that he had a unique and intriguing musical connection with his sister Bobbie."

Kris Kristofferson got behind the album, saying, "Ever true to his school and uncompromisingly true to himself, he has fashioned a body of work that is at once traditional and absolutely original, appealing to rockers and farmers, bikers and lawyers, blue collar and no collar."

Rolling Stone's esteemed reviewer David Fricke particularly enjoyed Willie Nelson's vocal prowess and Gimble's sublime fiddle playing. He wrote in December 1996: "Nelson's singing, with its craggy humanity and ruminative ache, remains a heavy wonder in itself, and the exquisite fiddling of old Bob Wills sidekick Johnny Gimble is always something to behold."

meantime [producer] Don Was is a good friend of Island Records chairman Chris Blackwell, and Don wanted to do a lot of Willie Nelson songs reggae style. We decided, why don't we experiment? We took our money and did our own reggae song. We took our musicians and an obscure song of mine from the 1970s, and we went to Jamaica to talk about the reggae album."

Nelson had a wonderful visit, staying at Golden Eye, the former home of James Bond author Ian Fleming, and set about dealing with Chris Blackwell. "I just had the greatest time, sitting around doing nothing but listen to music. I played Chris the song for the reggae album, which he liked." Nelson, seeing his opportunity, then asked Blackwell to have a listen to the new minimalist recordings that meant so much to him. "Then I played him, the whole *Spirit* album and he said. 'Yeah I want that too.'"

So, in April 1996, after being regarded as something of a has-been, Nelson became the first country music artist to sign with Island Records. Island Records may not have been as big a conglomerate as Sony, but its reputation as a progressive home for a long list of iconic rock, pop, and reggae acts was stellar. Founded by Blackwell in 1959 to give reggae a mainstream voice (Blackwell produced Bob Marley and the Wailers himself, and worked with Jimmy Cliff, Burning Spear, Steel Pulse, Black Uhuru, and many other top reggae outfits), Island launched quality music with the likes of Free, Cat Stevens, Linda Thompson, Fairport Convention, Traffic, Bad Company, King Crimson, the Chieftains, Roxy Music, Brian Eno, Sparks, Grace Jones, Marianne Faithfull, Tom Waits, and a four-piece Dublin band that called themselves U2.

In July 1989, Blackwell sold Island Records and Island Music to the PolyGram UK Group for a massive sum, reportedly in excess of $300 million, and Blackwell stayed on as president of the label for a few years, in which time he gave Nelson his seal of approval. The deal was innovative musically and in its marketing strategy. Nelson was to release two separate albums with Island, the back-to-basics piano and guitar album in the summer, followed three months later by a Don Was–produced reggae album.

Island's marketing guru Andrew Kronfeld explained the tactics to *Billboard* magazine in April 1996: "The first record is geared towards an upper demo, the second towards a younger group. In tandem, we'll get both audiences."

The reggae album was initially delayed and then put aside by Island, as a series of ownership and personnel changes affected several slated releases. But Nelson stuck with the project and *Countryman* finally saw the light of day in 2005, on Lost Highway Records.

Nelson was in top form with *Spirit*, and with the reggae project temporarily dismantled, he followed his Island Records debut with another fine effort for his new label, 1998's glowingly reviewed *Teatro*, produced by the critically acclaimed rock producer Daniel Lanois. Country rock singer Emmylou Harris sang background on most of the tracks, effortlessly weaving her bluegrass-influenced melancholy with Nelson's own western-infused isolation.

The results, as *No Depression* magazine noted in October 1998, ensured another challenging and unique song collection from the maestro: "Her timing, while at

OPPOSITE

One of Willie's many supporting movie roles, here as professional fisherman Billy Pooler in the 1997 Joe Pesci and Danny Glover comedy *Gone Fishin'*.

FOLLOWING PAGES

Willie and singer-songwriter Beck performing together at Tweeter Center in Chicago, Illinois, October 1997.

first jarring—it's as if she's a half-beat behind Nelson—only heightens the feeling of dissolution that pervades the project. That, and the record's shambling rhythms and arcane instrumentation, helps make Nelson's latest something of an avant-country answer to the post-rock wonder, Latin Playboys."

To get inside Nelson's creative head, Lanois spent a long time riding the tour bus with the veteran singer, quizzing Nelson about his musical roots. It was all Django Reinhardt guitar and music for dancing, Nelson explained, Reinhardt being the legendary Belgian gypsy jazz musician who revolutionized guitar playing in the 1930s and '40s. With that in mind, Lanois chose to record in an old theater in Oxnard, California, and encouraged Nelson's Reinhardt-inspired guitar playing.

Nelson ended 1998 on a very high note, at the John F. Kennedy Center for the Performing Arts. Along with comedian Bill Cosby, composer and conductor Andre Previn, diplomat and actress Shirley Temple Black, and Broadway musical writing team John Kander and Fred Ebb, sixty-five-year-old Willie Nelson was awarded the highly prestigious Kennedy Center Honor for "his invaluable contribution to the arts." The televised presentation—attended by President and Mrs. Clinton—saw Nelson honored by actor Tommy Lee Jones before Dwight Yoakam, Lyle Lovett, and Kris Kristofferson played several Nelson tunes, including a special all-star version of "On the Road Again."

Teatro

TRACK LISTING

Ou Es-Tu, Mon Amour? (Where Are You, My Love?) ✳ I Never Cared for You ✳ Everywhere I Go ✳ Darkness on the Face of the Earth ✳ My Own Peculiar Way ✳ These Lonely Nights ✳ Home Motel ✳ The Maker ✳ I Just Can't Let You Say Goodbye ✳ I've Just Destroyed the World (I'm Living In) ✳ Somebody Pick Up My Pieces ✳ Three Days ✳ I've Loved You All Over the World ✳ Annie

RECORDED

Summer 1998

RELEASED

September 1, 1998

LABEL

Island

PERSONNEL

Willie Nelson (vocals, acoustic guitar, electric guitar) ✳ Emmylou Harris (background vocals on all tracks except 1, 6, 7 & 14) ✳ Daniel Lanois (Gibson Les Paul, bass guitar) ✳ Tony Mangurian (drums, percussion) ✳ Victor Indrizzo (drums, percussion) ✳ Bobbie Nelson (Wurlitzer electric piano, organ) ✳ Brian Griffiths (guitars, slide guitar, mandolin) ✳ Mickey Raphael (harmonica, bass harmonica) ✳ Brad Mehldau (vibraphone, piano) ✳ Malcolm Burn (organ) ✳ Jeffrey Green (drums, omnichord, keyboard) ✳ Cyril Neville (congas)

PRODUCER

Daniel Lanois

Released to great acclaim in 1998, *Teatro* was quite a departure, sonically, for Willie Nelson. The album was recorded in an old theater (hence the title of the album), and produced by in-demand sound guru Daniel Lanois, best known for developing rock band U2's deep aural layering and sonic moviescapes, and rebranding Bob Dylan in 1997 with the seminal *Time Out of Mind* album.

Country singer Emmylou Harris had worked with Lanois in 1995 on the outstanding *Wrecking Ball* album that brought her a new audience, and a vastly different sound. Lanois was the ideal producer to bring something new and unusual to Nelson's voice, playing style, and conceptual songwriting.

Willie Nelson, in turn, was happy to give Lanois almost complete production control, as he explained to *Stomp and Stammer* magazine in April 1999. "I left it up to him, more or less, because his idea was to take the song, and the voice and the guitar and then build around it and enhance it. I was interested to see what he would do, so I let him have a free hand. We started out with 100 songs, picked twenty of those, and then ten of those to record. I turned in new songs and old songs together. And I felt like maybe all the new songs would get recorded, but I was going to let Daniel choose the ones he liked. He listened to the old ones and the new ones not knowing which was which, and he picked the songs that are on the album. I left it entirely up to him."

Rob Sheffield noted in the August 1998 edition of *Rolling Stone* that Nelson, on *Teatro*, "gets the Daniel Lanois treatment, singing old, new, borrowed and blue tunes amid Lanois' big drums and murky echo. As usual, Lanois overdoes the schlock atmospherics, but like Bob Dylan on *Time Out of Mind*, Nelson is earthy enough to keep Lanois in line."

6

2000 ✦ 2016

Roll Me Up

True to form, in 2000 Willie Nelson welcomed the new millennium with yet another musical surprise. Instead of continuing on a rock crossover path, the country stalwart stepped back and sideways for a potpourri of assorted blues with the eclectic but focused *Milk Cow Blues*. The collaborative project, released on Island Records, saw Nelson jam with blues contemporaries B. B. King and Dr. John, as well as members of a younger generation of blues artists including, Susan Tedeschi, Kenny Wayne Shepherd, and Jonny Lang. Country fans were a shade baffled by it, but the music press adored Nelson's blues adventure. *Rolling Stone*'s Parke Puterbaugh wrote: "The show belongs to Nelson, who has fashioned from these blues a sagebrush poet's autumnal meditation on faded love and the wages of the sporting life."

American roots music publication *No Depression* also loved the record, noting: "No matter how far afield the music takes him, Willie sounds very much at home, his conversational phrasing seemingly incapable of artifice, his guitar providing the same sort of punctuation to these tracks that it has on his country classics. For Nelson, it's all just music, this vast expanse of American song that he has somehow claimed as his own."

In the aftermath of the IRS problems and subsequent settlement, and knowing that all his albums sold in decent numbers, Nelson was quick to keep product on the shelves. With this in mind, prior to *Milk Cow Blues* he rushed out another quickie on his own label, Luck Records, *Tales Out of Luck (Me and the Drummer)*. Originally intended as an Internet-only release entitled *Me and the Drummer*, it featured Willie Nelson and the Offenders—a unit he'd first played with in 1966— with Jimmy Day on pedal steel guitar, fiddler Johnny Gimble, Johnny Bush on drums, Dave Zettner on bass, guitarists Clint Strong and Freddy Powers, and Floyd Domino on piano. It was a solidly country-and-western take on old Nelson material, most of it relatively unknown and previously unreleased.

RAINBOW CONNECTION

Next up, Nelson surprised everyone—except his daughter Amy, who as a huge Muppets fan had been urging Nelson to have a go at a children's record. So, in 2001, Willie Nelson released *Rainbow Connection*, again on Island Records, featuring a set of children's classic tunes. Trying to match Kermit's rendition of the oh-so-cheesy "Rainbow Connection" (written by hit songwriter Paul Williams), Nelson is simply masterful as the king of off-beat phrasing.

"I'm Looking Over a Four-Leaf Clover" is a bouncy sing-along, and Nelson allows Amy to shine on her version of "Rock Me to Sleep." And then Nelson, seemingly tired of the children's theme, slips in some typical melancholy on side two of the album with "Playin' Dominoes and Shootin' Dice."

Slate magazine admired his work on the offbeat album, claiming on March 4, 2005, that "Nelson is capable of redeeming the worst schlock, locating the kernel of real feeling in the most absurd material. Listen to him lagging teasingly behind the beat in *Rainbow Connection*, and to the truly lovely succession of notes he hits."

LOST HIGHWAY

Country music sales, according to many industry observers, had been inflated through the 1990s by the unique commercial success of Garth Brooks. Certainly the genre had gained in popularity, with other acts benefitting as a consequence, but Brooks was the real driving force behind the dramatic boom. And then, in October 2000, Garth Brooks retired to spend more time with his family and rode off to his ranch Oklahoma, leaving country music in a more vulnerable position.

ABOVE

Willie Nelson on the set of
his video for the song "Maria
(Shut Up and Kiss Me)," at the
Red Rock Saloon in New York
City, May 15, 2002.

Sales did drop, and by 2001 country music's share of music sales was just over 10 percent, down drastically from the 18.75 percent of just seven years before. Given the sales challenge, Nashville's more open-minded and forward-thinking executives, like Luke Lewis at Universal Music, recognized that the genre had to keep changing. In 2001, he and Frank Callari, manager of country rock band the Mavericks, started a Universal imprint called Lost Highway Records.

Lewis had been childhood friend of Gram Parsons in Florida. Parsons, the troubled country-loving rock-and-roller who attempted a country-rock fusion with the Byrds, the Flying Burrito Brothers, and his solo outfits, was the ultimate music maverick, dying at the age of twenty-six. This was the kind of music, and the kind of edgy personality, that Lewis understood and recognized as being able to make a mark in the country, rock, and pop markets.

On its inception, Highway Records started off with a bang, releasing the folksy bluegrass soundtrack from the movie *O Brother Where Art Thou?* and watching it sell nearly eight million copies in the United States alone, according to *Billboard* magazine. Artists on Lost Highway needed to have personality, musical originality, and a belief in their own path—so Lewis and Callari signed a young man many hailed as the new Gram Parsons, Ryan Adams, as well as one of country music's greatest mavericks of all time, Willie Nelson.

Nelson, no slouch at understanding the music industry, was already aware of the business changes in the air for country musiuc, telling Jennifer Ordonez of the *Wall Street Journal* in 2001, "Country music every now and then just sort of overproduces itself. Eventually the traditional artists come back. In my time I've seen it happen in two or three different cycles. The cream always rises back to the top."

Lewis explained to *Billboard* in their December 17, 2001 issue how he managed to maneuver Nelson from Universal-owned label Island to Lost Highway. "I begged for it. That's pretty much how it happened. It made my year just knowing he's here." *Billboard* also asked Nelson about his impressions of his new label. "Lost Highway has a great staff working for them . . . They are coming off a huge hit with *O Brother, Where Art Thou?* and they've done a great job with that."

THE GREAT DIVIDE

Willie's first album for Lost Highway was another genre buster, *The Great Divide*, which saw Nelson perform at his absolute best alongside contemporary rockers, including Sheryl Crow on "Be There for You," Bonnie Raitt on "You Remain," Brian McKnight on "Don't Fade Away," and rock-rap bad boy Kid Rock on "Last Stand in Open Country."

When *Billboard*'s Nashville correspondent Deborah Evans Price previewed the album, it was obvious that he was back on form. She wrote, "Upon a casual listen, Willie Nelson's forthcoming Lost Highways album, *The Great Divide*, sounds like it could be pages ripped from the *Red Headed Stranger*'s road-worn journal. Themes of passionate rebellion, relationship discord, and the consequences of time are as comfortable to Nelson as a weathered bandanna."

As he had done previously with rock producer Daniel Lanois, Nelson allowed producer Matt Serletic to have control during the album's production process, as he told *Billboard*: "I turned it over to Matt and let him run the whole show. When you take on a producer you have to let him drive the bus. That's what I did with him. You have to have confidence that he knows what he's doing, and I had that confidence." Serletic, talking to OnlineAthens.com in February 2002, said that Nelson was the "Premier duet partner of all time, been doing this a long time, so it's not really a new phenomenon that's been applied to him."

Nelson told in *Billboard* in 2001: "Someone told me the other day that I was

OPPOSITE

Willie performing the video for "Maria (Shut Up and Kiss Me)," from his 2002 album *The Great Divide*.

BELOW

Willie in June 2002, indulging
in one of his favorite pastimes,
a round of golf.

in the *Guinness Book of World Records* for doing more duets than anybody else in history. I don't doubt it. I like to sing with other singers. There was a time when it was difficult to do because of label restrictions. When Waylon Jennings and I got together and did our stuff, he was on RCA, and I was on another label. It was really the first sort of outlaw movement. It's nice to know we can do it openly now with blessings of most of the record companies."

Some less-than-conscientious critics were concerned that since the album only contained one new Nelson tune, the master craftsman was running out of

steam as a writer. The one new song he did contribute, however, was so good that accusation of wells running dry were ridiculously premature. Reviewing Willie's UK concert at the Royal Albert Hall in London, in June 2002, the *Guardian* pop critic John Aizelwood remarked most positively on the quality of Nelson's song "Great Divide": "A solitary co-songwriting credit on his current album, *The Great Divide*, suggests his writing powers are on the wane, yet the song in question, the title track itself, is imbued with Nelson's trademarks: yearning, regret and stoicism. It slots in imperiously towards the end of a 150-minute set."

And *Rolling Stone* raved: "The troubled Spanish acoustic of the title song makes it clear Nelson never needed the young blood that appears elsewhere on the record: Nelson's sound is so deep, so sad yet unapologetic, that he can make a lyric about the summer sun seem as dark and cold as a meditation on the Arctic."

"THEMES OF PASSIONATE REBELLION, RELATIONSHIP DISCORD, AND THE CONSEQUENCES OF TIME ARE AS COMFORTABLE TO NELSON AS A WEATHERED BANDANNA." —DEBORAH EVANS PRICE, *BILLBOARD*

Aside from musical endeavors, the early years of the new millennium saw the veteran entertainer spending more and more time in Maui playing golf and maintaining his good health with daily exercise. As he told the *Chicago Tribune* in 2005: "I do what I feel like doing. I don't have a rigid plan. If I don't feel like running, I'll do kicks. Each day is a little different, so I don't get bored. I try to mix it up." By kicks, Nelson was referring to his long-time participation in martial arts. It was something he had begun to take semi-seriously in Nashville in the 1960s, and then again in the '90s.

He took up taekwondo after his sons became enthusiasts and worked with Master Sam Um. In 2002, he earned a black belt in the Korean martial art, which left Johnny Cash less than impressed, as Nelson told Richard Skanse of *Lone Star Music* magazine in 2002: "Kris [Kristofferson] was telling them about my black belt and John was saying, 'Oh, that ain't nothing—I know a 74-year-old woman with a black belt.' So I told 'em 'Bring her on!'"

RIGHT

Live and Kickin', Willie's seventieth birthday concert, televised May 26, 2002, on USA Network. Here, Willie performs with ZZ Top.

FOLLOWING PAGES

Elvis Costello (right), one of the *Live and Kickin'* lineup, with his celebrated wife, Diana Krall, on piano, and Willie.

Nelson even took part in a taekwondo movie, *Evidence*, telling Skanse, "It was a lot of fun, because I did it with a lot of my friends there. I go to that school there, the Master of Martial Arts School in Austin. So I was just playing and having fun with a lot of friends. I don't know how the movie turned out, but I had fun."

That's not to say that Nelson was idle as he approached his seventieth birthday. He continued to work on the Don Was reggae project and dug back into his past again for his next Lost Highway album. That was *Run That by Me One More Time*, a duet album with an old employer from the 1960s, Ray Price, who had taken Nelson on as part of his famed Cherokee Cowboy Band back in 1961.

LIVE AND KICKIN'

Willie Nelson would turn seventy in April 2003, an event marked by cable television's USA Network when it announced on March 26 that the "legend and American icon" would be "joined by some of the biggest names in music for the special concert event, *Willie Nelson & Friends: Live and Kickin'*, an all-star lineup that will come together and perform in celebration of Willie's seventieth birthday in the two-hour telecast to air exclusively on USA Network on Memorial Day, Monday, May 26."

Elizabeth Porter Hogan, vice president of USA Network, said, "We are thrilled to be able to help Willie celebrate his birthday in such spectacular fashion. We've gathered together some of today's most exciting names in music."

Indeed they had. The concert, taped on Wednesday, April 10, 2003, at New York's Beacon Theatre, featured a multi-genre superstar lineup that included Ray Charles, Paul Simon, Kenny Chesney, Eric Clapton, John Mellencamp, Shelby Lynne, ZZ Top, Ray Price, Toby Keith, Shania Twain, Sheryl Crow, Norah Jones, Wyclef Jean, Elvis Costello, Diana Krall, Kris Kristofferson, Steven Tyler, and Lyle Lovett.

Eric Clapton brought some world-weary blues guitar and dusty vocals as he sang "Night Life" with Willie Nelson. Paul Simon rattled through "Homeward Bound," and Diana Krall and Elvis Costello worked up a jazzy take on Nelson's classic "Crazy."

Alternative country singer Shelby Lynne showcased Nelson's lilting "Angel Flying Too Close to the Ground," while country superstar Shania Twain surprised everyone who thought her just a manufactured pop diva, with a pitch-perfect and impassioned take on Nelson's beautiful ballad "Blue Eyes Crying in the Rain."

Aerosmith's Steven Tyler rocked out "Once Is Enough," ZZ Top kept it loud and upbeat with "She Loves My Automobile," and it was down to Wyclef Jean to change the mood with a delightful reggae version of "To All the Girls I've Loved Before."

Just to boost that already impressive star power and to give Nelson his due respect on a major birthday celebration, the performances were introduced by yet more A-listers: Ethan Hawke, Robert De Niro, Whoopi Goldberg, and one ex-president of the United States, Bill Clinton. Clinton got into the spirit of the evening after receiving some boos from the crowd, putting that down to them being "probably Republicans." He also joked to Willie Nelson, "Was that you with me on the roof?" referencing the by-then mythical tale that Nelson puffed on a joint or two on the roof of the White House when President Carter was in office in 1976.

The climax of the four-hour concert came at the end of the evening when the backing group for the musical guests was replaced by Willie's band, and they and Nelson sailed through top-notch renditions of "Whiskey River" and the Hank Williams classic "Jambalaya (On the Bayou)."

Shania Twain and Toby Keith then brought a guitar-shaped birthday cake onstage for the special guest, and all the attendees burst into an all-star version of "Happy Birthday" before finishing the evening with, of course, "On the Road Again."

IT ALWAYS WILL BE

In April 2004, Willie released a very personal jazz and pop-standard album, *Nacogdoches*, with his old friend and Fort Worth mentor Paul Buskirk. Nelson chose to make the production of his next album as easy on himself as possible—excusable, given his age and exhausting road schedule.

Producer James Stroud understood how to get the best out of Nelson, as Willie explained to David Freeland of *American Songwriter* in January 2007: "James and I, we had this formula that kind of worked. I would sing the song three times in a row, never listening to any playbacks, and then go to the next song. The theory is that the track is good and I know the song, so there's no need hanging around. We did twenty songs the first day and then played nine holes of golf!"

James Stroud steered 2004's *It Always Will Be* project from Music City with his own A-list musicians, and oversaw some terrific duets, notably Willie with daughter Paula on "Be That as It May," Americana icon Lucinda Williams on "Over Time," country hitmaker Toby Keith on the Allman Brothers classic "Midnight Rider," and the acclaimed jazz vocalist Norah Jones (whose style Nelson adored as soon as she burst on the scene) on "Dreams Come True."

The record drew excellent reviews around the world. Sue Keogh of the BBC said, "After more than five decades of recording, Shotgun Willie is still teaching the young country pups a thing or two about finding your own unique style and using it to impart a real depth of emotion to the listener."

Outlaws and Angels was essentially the soundtrack to another all-star Willie Nelson TV special, recorded in May 2004 at the Wiltern Theatre in Los Angeles. A magnificent lineup was assembled for Willie, including Bob Dylan, Keith Richards, Al Green, Carole King, Joe Walsh, Lucinda Williams, Kid Rock, Ben Harper, Rickie Lee Jones, Jerry Lee Lewis, and Toby Keith, who all performed tracks from the vast Willie Nelson catalogue.

The 2005 Don Was–produced *Countryman* album, a reggae-styled project that first got Nelson signed to Island Records by Chris Blackwell during a visit to Jamaica, had been an on-and-off affair for a long time. It took almost a decade to record from start to finish, and the finished album sounded patchy—perhaps not surprising considering its production time frame. Despite a few offbeat winners,

OPPOSITE

Country singer Patty Griffin,

taking part in the Tsunami

Relief Austin to South Asia

benefit concert, January 2005.

like a cool take on Johnny Cash's "Worried Man" in tandem with reggae master Toots Hibbert, and a better-than-average version of Jimmy Cliff's tough but melodic "The Harder They Come," for Nelson it seemed like an experiment that didn't quite have the passion to make it work.

ACTIVIST

The day after Christmas 2004, a magnitude 9.1 earthquake hit the Indian Ocean near Indonesia. The terrible result was a series of tsunamis that killed a staggering 230,000 people or more in over fourteen different countries, one of the most horrific and deadly natural disasters in history. Within days Willie Nelson was headlining a Texas benefit concert to raise money for victims of the tsunamis across southern Asia and eastern Africa. The concert was put together by the Austin musician Michael Hall, who called Nelson as soon as he came up with a plan. "I started at the top," he told the *Associated Press* January 4, 2005, "and when Willie said 'Count me in,' I knew we were off and running."

"AFTER MORE THAN FIVE DECADES OF RECORDING, SHOTGUN WILLIE IS STILL TEACHING THE YOUNG COUNTRY PUPS A THING OR TWO ABOUT FINDING YOUR OWN UNIQUE STYLE AND USING IT TO IMPART A REAL DEPTH OF EMOTION TO THE LISTENER" —SUE KEOGH, BBC

The Tsunami Relief Austin to South Asia concert took place on January 9, 2005, at the Austin Music Hall with—alongside Nelson—Patty Griffin, Spoon, Joe Ely, Bruce Robison and Kelly Willis, and Alejandro Escovedo. Every single artist donated their time freely, and the concert raised over $75,000 for UNICEF, the American Red Cross, and Doctors without Borders. More cash was raised when the DVD *Willie Nelson Songs for Tsunami Relief: Austin to South Asia* was released.

In 2004, Nelson's wife—like her husband a long-time environmentalist— bought herself a diesel car in Hawaii that could be powered by biodiesel. Annie

Nelson drove the new car to Pacific Biodiesel, the Maui biodiesel fuel pump in Kahului, filled up, and was amazed at the results.

Nelson explained the importance of the event to *New York Times* writer Danny Hakim in December 2005: "I drove the car, loved the way it drove. The tailpipe smells like French fries. I bought me a Mercedes, and the Mercedes people were a little nervous when I took a brand new Mercedes over and filled it up with 100 percent vegetable oil coming from the grease traps of Maui. I figured I'd be getting notices about the warranty and that stuff. However, nobody said anything. I get better gas mileage, it runs better, the motor runs cleaner, so I swear by it,"

Biodiesel fuel is made from vegetable oil (mainly soybean oil), and can be used without any automobile adaptation or extra parts on regular diesel engines. Excited at the potential of this new fuel, Nelson and Annie found some partners who were also interested in the possibilities of this new clean fuel form, mostly for America's truck drivers, and formed a company, Willie Nelson's Biodiesel, to establish biodiesel sales at truck stops across the country. Nelson was already using biodiesel on his own cars and tour buses. As he said in a press release, "There is really no need going around starting wars over oil. We have it here at home. We have the necessary product, the farmers can grow it."

As far as the economic power of the fuel, Nelson told Hakim, "I hope somebody makes money out of it; I'm sure they will. And probably what'll happen is that the oil industry will wait until everybody else builds all the infrastructure and then they'll come in and take over. But that's O.K. I don't worry about that. As along as the idea progresses because all I'm caring about is getting it out there and maybe helping the country, the farmer, the environment."

Much of Nelson's environmental activism springs from his sense of injustice over many issues, from the racism he witnessed on the road in the 1960s to feeling victimized and targeted as an outspoken supporter and user of marijuana. He was first arrested for cannabis possession in 1974, and others followed, but the arrest in 2006 bothered the normally laissez-faire Nelson more than most.

On September 18, 2006, Nelson was on his bus traveling through Louisiana on his way to the funeral of Texas governor Ann Richards, a good friend over the years. Police pulled the bus over and searched it after detecting a strong smell of marijuana. They found one and a half pounds of marijuana and three ounces of mushrooms on the bus. Nelson avoided jail but did receive six months of probation. "Both bus drivers were over 50 years old," Nelson said, dryly, in a statement. "The other guys were 60 years old. My sister is 75, I'm 73, so it's like they busted an old folks home."

On a more serious note, Nelson continued to speak out from his position on the advisory board for the National Organization for the Reform of Marijuana Laws, "It's a matter of time," Nelson noted in 2008, "a matter of education, a matter of people finding out what cannabis, marijuana is for, why it grows out of the ground, and why it's prescribed as one of the greatest stress medicines on the planet."

BELOW

Willie's son Miles and the singer's three-year old grandson, Mason, refueling with Willie Nelson's own brand of biofuel, BioWillie, Wilmer, Texas, October 2006.

YOU DON'T KNOW ME

Cindy Walker, a "songwriter's songwriter," had long ago earned a special place in Willie Nelson's musical heart when he set about paying tribute to her craft in 2006 with the purest of pure country album *You Don't Know Me: The Songs of Cindy Walker.*

On the album Willie and the band sauntered through a host of Cindy Walker's western-flavored songs that they all grew up on in Texas. Walker had provided Nelson's western swing hero Bob Wills with numerous songs such as "Cherokee Maiden," "Dusty Skies," and "Bubbles in My Beer." She also gave Gene Autry (Nelson's favorite cowboy actor) "Blue Canadian Rockies," but she's probably best known as the creator of the all-time classic "You Don't Know Me," which has been recorded over the decades by a long list of multi-genre artists, including Elvis Presley, Ray Charles, Van Morrison, and Bette Midler.

Cindy Walker was born in 1918 in a small town in Texas called Mart. It was just forty miles from Nelson's hometown of Abbott. She started writing her own songs as a teenager and had carried a song with her that she dreamed Bing Crosby might record one day, when she went to Los Angeles with her family in 1940.

Fearless, or hopelessly naive, or maybe both, the twenty-two-year-old budding writer had her father stop outside the Crosby Building on Sunset Boulevard. She recounted the tale to the *Chicago Tribune* in 1988: "I had decided that if I ever got to Hollywood, I was going to try to show Bing Crosby a song I had written for him called 'Lone Star Trail.' My father said, 'You're crazy, girl,' but he stopped the car."

As fate would have it, Bing's brother Larry, the singer's publicity director, was in an amenable mood, and in a few minutes Cindy came back to her parents' car to get her mother to come inside and play piano for her. She had her chance to impress, and Larry liked it enough to set Cindy up with a meeting with Bing Crosby the next day at Paramount studios, where the superstar crooner was shooting scenes for a new movie. She sang her song to Crosby, Bing liked it, and he recorded it. It became the first of Walker's many hits over the next fifty years. When Nelson's friend and top songwriter Harlan Howard was inducted into the Country Music Hall of Fame in 1997, Howard said that fellow inductee Walker was simply "the greatest living songwriter of country music."

In a press release for his tribute album, Nelson wrote: "Cindy has written songs consistently over the years that have become traditional standards. That sets her aside from your normal, everyday writer. She affected me and everyone else who came along after her. We had to have heard her music before we could do ours."

Nelson's album brought attention back to Cindy Walker, a timely tribute to the songwriter who passed away just a few days after the official release of *You Don't Know Me: The Songs of Cindy Walker*. "I loved her dearly and will miss her. And I'm glad that the music came out while she could still enjoy it," Nelson said in a statement on hearing of Walker's death.

RINGING THE CHANGES

That same year, 2006, Willie went left field again by working with fellow Lost Highway artist Ryan Adams on a set of classic songs (original and otherwise) produced by the young alternative country star. *Songbird* was produced by Adams, with own band the Cardinals backing Nelson, although Nelson's harmonica player Mickey Raphael appeared on several tracks.

Nelson's next album saw him back in more familiar territory for the appropriately titled double CD *Last of the Breed*, with fellow traditional country

BELOW

Willie and Annie D'Angelo
Nelson at the unveiling
ceremony of a Willie Nelson
statue in Austin, Texas, on
June 20, 2012.

survivors Merle Haggard and Ray Price. *Pitchfork* magazine, delighted with the trio's vocal integrity, especially in combination, wrote on March 30, 2007, that "they sound best on Kristofferson's 'Why Me.' That song has always seemed like a solitary prayer (especially on Johnny Cash's lonely *American Recordings* version), but sung by a veteran trio, it almost sounds like a career retrospective, as if they're humbled by their large audience, long legacies, and close friendship."

True to his eclectic nature, Nelson then went down a jazz path for his next record, a unique collaboration with trumpet star Wynton Marsalis on *Two Men with the Blues*, a live album that was well received by jazz critics and topped the *Billboard* Jazz Albums chart.

Nelson's career has been filled with assorted collaborations, blending his voice and music with an array of diverse talents, but even those used to his wandering ways were surprised by his 2008 recording with rap artist (and celebrated weed fan) Snoop Dogg.

Songbird

TRACKS

Rainy Day Blues ✳ Songbird ✳ Blue Hotel ✳
Back to Earth ✳ Stella Blue ✳ Hallelujah ✳ $1000
Wedding ✳ We Don't Run ✳ Yours Love ✳ Sad
Songs and Waltzes ✳ Amazing Grace

RECORDED

Summer 2006

RELEASED

October 31, 2006

LABEL

Lost Highway Records

PERSONNEL

Willie Nelson (acoustic guitar, vocals) ✳ Ryan Adams
(acoustic guitar, electric guitar, bass guitar) ✳ Jon
Graboff (pedal steel) ✳ Brad Pemberton (drums) ✳
Neal Casal (piano, guitar) ✳ Catherine Popper (bass
guitar) ✳ Mickey Raphael (harmonica) ✳ Glenn Patscha
(Hammond B-3) ✳ Melonie Daniels (choir) ✳ Darius
Booker (choir) ✳ Tiffany Palmer (choir) ✳ Karen Bernod
(choir) ✳ Felicia Graham (choir) ✳ Horace V. Rogers
(choir) ✳ Carlos Ricketts (choir and choir arranger)

PRODUCER

Ryan Adams

Ryan Adams—country's best-known bad boy since Gram Parsons—was an odd choice to produce Nelson's 2006 album, *Songbird,* despite being a label mate of Nelson's at the progressive Lost Highway label.

The album featured some unusual covers, from Gram Parson's "$1000 Wedding" to the title track, Christine McVie's "Songbird," and Leonard Cohen's rousing "Hallelujah." Adams came up with a sizzling take of Willie Nelson's old classics "Rainy Day Blues" and "We Don't Run," but it was the new songs—"Back to Earth," from Nelson and Adams's "Blue Hotel"—that really lifted the collection to something interesting and worthy of a serious listen.

Nelson told David Freeland of *American Songwriter* magazine in 2007, that he was intrigued by Adams. "I love him to death," Nelson said, "I think he's a great artist. Naturally, he's a little weird; we all gotta be a little weird to be in this kind of business anyway, but his weirdness is associated with a lot of ingenious things that he's doing."

Unfortunately, reviewers weren't all taken by Adams's production, with *Rolling Stone*'s Robert Christgau writing "Adams loves his band the Cardinals very much, and Nelson is an affable fellow. But the Cardinals' indistinct country-rock hybrid muffles the material."

The album was Lost Highway founder Luke Lewis's idea, Nelson told David Freeland of *American Songwriter*: "It was Luke [who] suggested we get together and do something, and I respect Luke a lot. I wasn't that familiar with Ryan, to be honest with you. . . . His sound was, as everybody knows, a little different from what mine is, but we managed to come together well."

"You know, me and Snoop smoke a lot," Nelson told CNN's Piers Morgan in 2012. "I was in Amsterdam one time and Snoop called me and wanted me to sing on his record. And I said, 'OK.' He said, 'Where are you?' And I said, 'I'm in Amsterdam.' So he caught the next plane and came over. And we recorded a song together." The song was Snoop's "My Medicine," with Snoop rapping over a firm country beat provided by a fellow rapper and guitarist, and promoted via a video shot in Nashville.

Early in 2009, Willie played it a bit safer again, recording a fine Texas swing album with western swing specialists Asleep at the Wheel, entitled *Willie and the Wheel.* Then after spending some time in the fall hanging out and playing dominoes with actor buddies Owen Wilson and Woody Harrelson in Hawaii, he headed back to an appointment in Nashville with a new label, Rounder, and a new producer, T Bone Burnett, for what he described as his very first traditional album, called, simply enough, *Country Music.*

The record saw Nelson and a top-flight bluegrass combo play classic tunes like "Dark as a Dungeon," "Freight Train Boogie," "Pistol Packin' Mama," and "Satisfied Mind." Nelson told the *Boot*, on the album's release in 2010, that Burnett "brought some great songs, put together some good musicians and then it was up to us. I knew the songs, so I just started singing and listening to everybody around me play. It was a great experience to know that anywhere I looked there would be a great musician to take the course."

On May 26, 2010, it was reported that Willie Nelson had cut his famous locks. The Nashville celebrity journalist Jimmy Carter posted a photo of Nelson without his trademark pigtails—evidently Nelson just wanted a more manageable hairstyle. And while fashion statements of the stars of the day are commonplace in the entertainment columns, for a seventy-seven-year-old to make the news for cutting his hair it was certainly unusual—and a testament to the place Nelson occupied in popular culture, even in 2010.

HEROES

What goes around comes around, and in 2012, almost twenty years after parting ways with Sony, Nelson was back with the company via the Legacy Recording division of Sony Music.

The deal involved both new recordings and archive material that Nelson would review and approve himself from his Columbia and RCA catalogues. His first release for Legacy was a country-meets-jazz-meets-Texas swing album titled *Heroes*, in which Nelson again worked with a host of all-star and cross-genre guest artists, including Jamey Johnson, Merle Haggard, Sheryl Crow, Ray Price, Snoop Dogg, and Kris Kristofferson.

One highlight was the witty "Roll Me Up and Smoke Me When I Die," with Willie joined by Kristofferson, Johnson, and Snoop Dogg. *People* magazine

OPPOSITE

Neil Young with Willie on

Nelson's eightieth birthday TV

special for CMT's *Crossroads.*

awarded the album 3.5 out of 4, summing it all up with "The iconic outlaw saddles up with some worshipful fans . . . showing his eternal cool."

Most interesting for Nelson was the impact made by his son, Lukas, who played guitar or sang on most tracks on the album. Lukas had left his home in Hawaii to attend university in California. He dropped out of college and began his music career in 2008 with drummer Anthony LoGerfo, forming a band called Promise of the Real. The band supported Nelson on several tours, made some indie recordings, and continued to pay their dues until breaking through with the 2012 album, *Wasted.* The *Austin Chronicle* raved, "There's an identifiable vibe, not unlike the one the Band had."

In a press statement about *Heroes,* Lukas said, "I love when I get a chance to duet and sing harmony with my dad. We do sing a lot together. And, I really liked the Eddie Vedder song we did ("Just Breathe"). I ran into Eddie, and he said he heard it and he gave me big love and hugged me."

" 'HEROES' KIND OF WINDS UP SUMMARIZING ALL THAT'S GOOD AND BAD ABOUT WILLIE AS HE APPROACHES HIS 80TH BIRTHDAY: HE'S OPEN TO EVERYTHING BUT HAS NO INNATE EDITOR, SO HE WHIFFS AS OFTEN AS HE CONNECTS, BUT WHEN HE DOES CONNECT, IT'S A WONDER TO BEHOLD."

—STEPHEN THOMAS ERLEWINE, ALLMUSIC.COM

OCTOGENARIAN

His eightieth birthday in April 2013 saw Nelson release another album of American standards and country classics, *Let's Face the Music and Dance,* with songs from composers as varied as Irving Berlin (the title song), Carl Perkins

("Matchbox"), and Django Reinhardt ("Nuages"). Also marking his eightieth year
was a special edition of Country Music Television's *Crossroads* featuring "Willie
Nelson & Friends" with a lineup including longtime fans Jack White, Sheryl
Crow, Jamey Johnson, Norah Jones, Ashley Monroe, Leon Russell, and Neil Young.

   Willie continued to ride high through the landmark year, with one of the
most high-powered collaboration albums of his career, *To All the Girls . . .*, a set

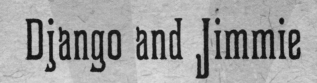

Django and Jimmie

TRACK LISTING

Django and Jimmie ✳ It's All Going to Pot ✳ Unfair
Weather Friend ✳ Missing Ol' Johnny Cash ✳ Live This
Long ✳ Alice in Hulaland ✳ Don't Think Twice, It's All Right
✳ Family Bible ✳ It's Only Money ✳ Swinging Doors ✳
Where Dreams Come to Die ✳ Somewhere Between ✳
Driving the Herd ✳ The Only Man Wilder Than Me

RECORDED

Spring 2015

RELEASED

June 2, 2015

LABEL

Legacy Recordings

PERSONNEL

Willie Nelson, Bobby Bare, Jamey Johnson, Merle Haggard
(vocals) ✳ Eddie Bayers, Tony Creasman, Lonnie Wilson
(drums) ✳ Eli Beaird (bass guitar) ✳ Willie Nelson, Larry
Brown (piano) ✳ Renato Caranto (saxophone) ✳ Dan
Dugmore (steel guitar) ✳ Kevin "Swine" Grantt (bass guitar,
upright bass) ✳ Ben Haggard (electric guitar) ✳ Tony
Harrell (keyboards) ✳ Mike Johnson (acoustic slide guitar,
dobro, steel guitar) ✳ Alison Krauss, Liana Manis, Wyatt
Beard, Melonie Cannon (background vocals) ✳ Catherine
Styron Marx (Hammond B-3 organ, piano) ✳ Mickey Raphael
(harmonica) ✳ Bobby Terry (acoustic guitar, electric guitar)

PRODUCER

Buddy Cannon

"Me and Merle got a new album called *Django and Jimmie* and the title track is about Django Reinhardt and Jimmie Rodgers," Willie Nelson announced to the press ahead of the April 2015 launch of the collaborative recording: "Both of those guys were very influential in both of our careers."

Almost thirty years previously, Haggard and Nelson had made the seminal *Pancho & Lefty* album, and *Django and Jimmie*—featuring two wise and still feisty old masters—comes close to eclipsing that 1983 classic. Producer Buddy Cannon kept both maverick artists in check, and coaxed wonderful performances as they paid tribute to jazz guitarist Django Reinhardt and 1930s bluesy country pioneer Jimmie Rodgers.

But it's not all Django and Jimmie. While working on the album, touched by nostalgia, Haggard penned a heartfelt and warmly expressed tribute song to old buddy Johnny Cash, "Missing Ol' Johnny Cash."

There's also a deft reworking of Bob Dylan's "Don't Think Twice, It's Alright," and very cleverly the two old friends even pay tribute to each other, with Willie doing Merle's "Somewhere Between" and Haggard singing Nelson's "Family Bible."

The album is filled with humanity and warmth, elements visible on several promotional videos shot in the studio during the making of the album. NPR radio suggested in its review that the album will "lift the spirits of even the gloomiest listener."

of new duets with the absolute best of country and popular music's female artists, namely Dolly Parton, Mavis Staples, Sheryl Crow, Loretta Lynn, Wynonna Judd, Rosanne Cash, Alison Krauss, Miranda Lambert, Tina Rose, Carrie Underwood, Emmylou Harris, Norah Jones, the Secret Sisters, Brandi Carlile, Lily Meola, Shelby Lynne, and daughter Paula Nelson. The album, not surprisingly, entered the *Billboard* Country album chart at #2.

At the tender age of eighty-one, Willie Nelson was awarded a fifth-degree black belt in taekwondo and then watched excitedly as his latest album, *Band of Brothers*, which featured nine brand-new Nelson songs, went to #1 on the country album chart in June 2014.

Nelson made his next album with old friend and fellow country legend Merle Haggard. *Django and Jimmie* also made #1 on the *Billboard* country chart. Producer Buddy Cannon clearly adored every minute working with the two living legends, and letting them cut loose with the rip-roaring and truly amusing cannabis wordplay song "It's All Going to Pot." *Rolling Stone* concurred on the

BELOW

Merle Haggard and Willie in 2015, promoting the release of *Django and Jimmie*.

quality of the album and that witty ode to dope in particular, describing the album's punchy single as "Two masters nailing the right song at the right time."

"It's All Going to Pot," was a pleasant appetizer for Nelson's announcement that he was launching his own cannabis brand, Willie's Reserve, to be grown in Colorado and Washington. "I am looking forward to working with the best growers in Colorado and Washington to make sure our product is the best on the market," he announced.

Once again Nelson was on a roll, and after being honored with the Gershwin Prize for Popular Song by the Library of Congress in 2015, he recorded an album of Gershwin tunes, *Summertime: Willie Nelson Sings Gershwin* that went on to top the jazz charts in 2016.

Also in 2016, Nelson released *For the Good Times: A Tribute to Ray Price*, a warm tribute with Nelson covering some of Price's greatest tracks, including "Heartaches by the Number," "Crazy Arms," "Night Life," "Faded Love," and "For the Good Times." Willie also appeared in the Country Music Association fiftieth anniversary tribute *Forever Country*, which featured his song "On the Road Again."

If that wasn't enough, Nelson wrote and published a novel, *Pretty Paper*, a backstory to the song of the same name he wrote back in the early '60s about a disabled beggar he saw in Fort Worth. The song was a hit for Roy Orbison in 1963, and is now a fully fleshed out story with an inspiring ending.

In good health after a couple of bumps on the road during 2016, Willie Nelson is back to riding the bus and playing for his fans, planning new recordings, and appearing in movie cameos. He was pleasantly surprised on February 12, 2017, when the winners for the 59th Grammy Awards were announced, and his very personal Gershwin tribute, *Summertime: Willie Nelson Sings Gershwin*, won the award for Best Traditional Pop Vocal Album.

In good health after a couple of minor setbacks during 2016, Willie Nelson is back playing for his fans, with a new album, *God's Problem Child*, released on April 28, 2017. And he was pleasantly surprised on February 12, 2017, when the winners for the 59th Grammy Awards were announced, and *Summertime: Willie Nelson Sings Gershwin* won the award for Best Traditional Pop Vocal Album. Just the latest in the long line of achievements by one of country music's favorite sons, and a true American icon.

RECOMMENDED ALBUMS

And Then I Wrote (Liberty, 1962)

Here's Willie Nelson (Liberty, 1963)

Country Willie: His Own Songs (RCA, 1965)

Country Favorites—Willie Nelson Style (RCA, 1966)

Make Way for Willie Nelson (RCA, 1967)

The Party's Over (RCA, 1967)

Texas in My Soul (RCA, 1968)

Good Times (RCA, 1968)

My Own Peculiar Way (RCA, 1968)

Both Sides Now (RCA, 1970)

Laying My Burdens Down (RCA, 1970)

Willie Nelson and Family (RCA, 1971)

Yesterday's Wine (RCA, 1971)

The Words Don't Fit the Picture (RCA, 1972)

The Willie Way (RCA, 1972)

Shotgun Willie (Atlantic, 1973)

Phases and Stages (Atlantic, 1974)

Red Headed Stranger (Columbia, 1975)

The Sound in Your Mind (Columbia, 1976)

To Lefty from Willie (Columbia, 1978)

Stardust (Columbia, 1978)

Willie Nelson Sings Kristofferson (Columbia, 1979)

Pretty Paper (Columbia, 1979)

Somewhere over the Rainbow (Columbia, 1981)

Always on My Mind (Columbia, 1982)

Tougher Than Leather (Columbia, 1983)

Willie Nelson (Columbia box set, 1983)

Me and Paul (Columbia, 1985)

Willie Nelson: Lone Star (Classic Country, 1985)

Highwayman (with Johnny Cash, Waylon Jennings, Kris Kristofferson) (Columbia, 1985)

Half Nelson (Columbia, 1985)

Mellow Moods of the Vintage Years (82 Music, 1985)

Willie Nelson (RCA, 1985)

What a Wonderful World (Columbia, 1988)

A Horse Called Music (Columbia, 1989)

On the Road Again (Columbia, 1989)

Highwayman II (Columbia, 1990)

Born for Trouble (Columbia, 1990)

Yours Always (Columbia, 1990)

Who'll Buy My Memories? (The IRS Tapes) (Sony, 1991)

Across the Borderline (Sony, 1993)

Moonlight Becomes You (Justice, 1994)

Spirit (Island, 1996)

Teatro (Island, 1998)

Milk Cow Blues (Island, 2000)

Rainbow Connection (Island, 2001)

The Great Divide (Island) 2001

It Always Willie Be (Lost Highway, 2004)

Countryman (Lost Highway, 2005)

Songbird (Lost Highway, 2006)

Moment of Forever (Lost Highway, 2008)

American Classic (Lost Highway, 2009)

Country Music (Rounder, 200)

Heroes (Legacy, 2012)

Let's Face the Music and Dance, 2013)

To All the Girls (Legacy, 2013)

Band of Brothers (Legacy, 2014)

Summertime (Legacy, 2016)

For the Good Times: A Tribute to Ray Price (Legacy, 2016)

COLLABORATIVE ALBUMS

Wanted: The Outlaws, with Waylon Jennings, Jessi Colter, and Tompall Glaser (RCA, 1976)

Waylon and Willie, with Waylon Jennings (RCA, 1978)

One for the Road, with Leon Russell (Columbia, 1979)

Willie Nelson and Danny Davis & the Nashville Brass (RCA, 1980)

San Antonio Rose Ray Price (Columbia 1980)

WWII, with Waylon Jennings (RCA, 1982)

Old Friends, with Roger Miller (Columbia, 1982)

In the Jailhouse Now, with Webb Pierce (Columbia, 1982)

The Winning Hand, with Kris Kristofferson, Dolly Parton, and Brenda Lee (Monument 1982)

Pancho & Lefty, with Merle Haggard (Epic, 1983)

Take It to the Limit, with Waylon Jennings (Columbia, 1983)

Music from Songwriter, with Kris Kristofferson (Columbia, 1984)

Funny How Time Slips Away, with Faron Young (Columbia, 1985)

Brand on My Heart, with Hank Snow (Columbia, 1985)

Walking the Line, with Merle Haggard and George Jones (Epic, 1987)

Seashores of Old Mexico, with Merle Haggard (Epic, 1987)

Clean Shirt, with Waylon Jennings (Epic, 1991)

Augusta, with Don Cherry (Sundown, 1995)

Hill Country Christmas, with Bobbie Nelson (Finer Arts, 1997)

VH1 Storytellers: Johnny Cash & Willie Nelson (American Recordings. 1998)

Run That by Me One More Time, with Ray Price (Lost Highway, 2003)

Last of the Breed, with Merle Haggard and Ray Price (Lost Highway, 2007)

Two Men with the Blues, with Wynton Marsalis (Blue Note, 2008)

Willie and the Wheel, with Asleep at the Wheel (Bismeaux, 2009)

Willie's Stash, Vol. 1: December Day, with Bobbie Nelson (Legacy, 2014)

Django and Jimmie, with Merle Haggard (Legacy, 2015)

MOVIES

The Electric Horseman (1979)

Honeysuckle Rose (1980)

Thief (1981)

Coming out of the Ice (1982)

Barbarosa (1982)

Hells Angels Forever (1983)

Songwriter (1984)

Red Headed Stranger (1984)

Stagecoach (1986)

The Last Days of Frank and Jesse James (1986)

Once upon a Texas Train (1988)

Where the Hell's That Gold?!!? (1988)

Walking after Midnight (1988)

Pair of Aces (1990)

Wild Texas Wind (1991)

Another Pair of Aces: Three of a Kind (1991)

Big Dreams & Broken Hearts: The Dottie West Story (1995)

Starlight (1996)

Anthem (1997)

Wag the Dog (1997)

Gone Fishin' (1997)

Half Baked (1998)

Outlaw Justice (1999)

Dill Scallion (1999)

Austin Powers: The Spy Who Shagged Me (1999)

The Country Bears (2002)

The Big Bounce (2004)

The Dukes of Hazzard (2005)

Broken Bridges (2006)

The Unforeseen (2007)

Blonde Ambition (2007)

Surfer, Dude (2008)

Beer for My Horses (2008)

Swing Vote (2008)

The King of Luck (2011)

The Zen of Bennett (2012)

When Angels Sing (2013)

Waiting for the Miracle to Come (2015)

Zoolander 2 (2016)

BOOKS BY WILLIE NELSON

Pretty Paper (with David Ritz, Blue Rider Press, 2016)

It's a Long Story: My Life by Willie Nelson (with David Ritz, Back Bay Books, 2015)

Roll Me Up and Smoke Me When I Die: Musings from the Road (William Morrow 2013)

A Tale Out of Luck with Mike Blakely (Center Street, 2008)

The Tao of Willie: A Guide to the Happiness in Your Heart (with Turk Pipkin, Avery, 2007)

The Facts of Life and Other Dirty Jokes (Random House, 2002)

Willie: An Autobiography (with Bud Shrake, Cooper Square Press, 2000)

BIBLIOGRAPHY

Eric Bannister. *Johnny Cash FAQ: All That's Left to Know About the Man in Black.* Backbeat, 2014.

Tony Byworth. *The Definite Illustrated Encyclopedia of Country Music.* Flame Tree, 2006.

Colin Escott. *I Saw the Light: The Story of Hank Williams.* Back Bay, 2015.

Merle Haggard. *My House of Memories: For the Record.* Harper Entertainment, 2002.

Michael Kosser. *How Nashville Became Music City, USA.* Hal Leonard, 2006.

Rick Koster. *Texas Music.* St. Martin's Press, 2000.

Laurie Jasinski. *Handbook of Texas Music.* Texas State Historical Institution, 2013.

Bill C. Malone. *Country Music USA.* University of Texas Press, 2010.

Robert K. Oermann. *Behind the Grand Ole Opry Curtain.* Center Street, 2008.

Jan Reid. *Improbable Rise of Redneck Rock.* Eidelberg, 1974.

The Rolling Stone Illustrated History of Rock and Roll. Random House, 1992.

Michael Streissguth. *Outlaw: Waylon, Willie, Kris and the Renegades of Nashville.* It Books, 2014.

Geronimo Treviño III. *History of Texas Country Music.* Taylor Trade, 2002.

Andrew Vaughan. *Who's Who in New Country.* Omnibus, 1990.

Andrew Vaughan. *The World of Country Music.* Studio Editions, 2002.

Texas Monthly, Rolling Stone, Goldmine, People, theboot.com, cmt.com, tasteofcountry.com, nashcountrydaily, cmaworld.com

QUOTE SOURCES

Quotes by Willie Nelson unless otherwise indicated.

CHAPTER ONE

"I've always felt like Abbott was a special place . . ." *Texas Monthly*, December 2005.

"I started out with a thumb pick . . ." *Frets*, December 1984.

"Abbott was a little bitty picture of the whole world . . ." *Texas Monthly*, December 2005.

"Well, I heard everything . . ." PBS Oral Histories.

"I remember when we used to sit around and watch the radio . . ." *Goldmine*, January 1995.

"I think there's a big freedom in Texas" *Rolling Stone*, July 13, 1978.

"Whenever the operators would take a vacation . . ." *Texas Monthly*, December 2005.

"My test was to do fifteen minutes . . ." *Country Song Roundup*, February 1969.

"I learned to play guitar from an old colored man . . ." Hank Williams, *San Francisco Chronicle*, April 1951.

"Bob Wills was my hero in those days . . ." PBS (pbsamericanrootsmusic.com).

CHAPTER TWO

"You name it, I sold it . . ."
Daily Telegraph (UK), April 23, 2013.

"I am religious, even though . . ." *Rolling Stone*, July 13,
1978.

"I was taught by Paul Buskirk . . ."
Rolling Stone, September 30, 2004.

"Pappy had a good ear . . ."
Herb Remington, *Houston Press*, April 23, 2013.

"I told him I wasn't going to buy them . . ."
Larry Butler, *Houston Press*, April 24, 2013.

"Nashville's a small town now . . ."
Harlan Howard talking to author, 1988.

"If you missed a friend backstage . . ."
Jimmy Dickens, *Boot*, July 23, 2015.

"If they had dropped a bomb on Tootsie's . . ."
Bobby Bare, *Nashville Scene*, November 4, 2010.

"Tootsie's was always a kind of magic place . . ."
Tennessean, May 8, 1995.

"It was a time with Harlan Howard . . ."
Phoenix.com, January 2002.

"'Well, I'll go in there and talk to Hal . . .'"
Hank Cochran, International Songwriters' Association
blog, 2002.

"He placed me and two of my brothers . . ."
Billy Walker, billywalker.com.

"In 1955 . . . Elvis joined me for a tour . . ."
Billy Walker, billywalker.com.

"First of all, Donny Young . . ." *Billboard*, 2012.

"The faster I made it . . ."
WHYY-FM *Fresh Air* (National Public Radio), 1996.

"They had to do something to kind of fix it . . ."
Ray Price, *WHYY Fresh Air* (National Public Radio), 1999.

"I was a musician who had been educated . . ."
Chet Atkins, talking to author, 1990.

"It was a lot of fun . . ." *Goldmine*, February 1999.

"We were at Tootsie's . . ."
CMT Hot 20 Countdown, April 2015.

"Willie wrote and was writing . . ."
Paul Kingsbury, National Public Radio, 2000.

CHAPTER THREE

"Willie was just so good . . ."
Chet Atkins, talking to author, 1990.

"In Nashville they didn't understand . . ."
Kris Kristofferson, *Texas Monthly*, May 2008.

"I didn't feel like I failed in Nashville . . ."
Parade.com, June 2010.

"I started making the papers in 1956 . . ."
Paul English, Savingcountrymusic.com, October 2009.

"I played around when I was pretty young . . ."
Playboy, November 2002.

"People never believe me . . ."
Charley Pride, *Houston Press*, April 25, 2012.

"I had a session set up . . ."
Jack Clement, *No Depression*, August 5, 2004.

"It was like a reverse of what happened with Elvis . . ."
Jack Clement, talking to author, 1990.

"We figured if they just listened to how good . . ."
Chet Atkins, talking to author, 1990.

"He'd been treated unfairly . . ." *Parade*, June 24, 2010.

"By the time I got there, it was burning real good . . ."
People, September 1, 1980.

"It was a very loose time . . ."
Norman Blake, talking to author, 2010.

"I turned to an old blue collegiate dictionary . . ."
Hazel Smith, CMT documentary *American Revolutions:
Wanted the Outlaws.*

"When Woodstock happened . . ." *Texas Monthly*, April 2012.

"The three masters of rubato . . ."
Jerry Wexler, *Texas Monthly*, May 2008.

"Otherwise, I would've had to aim to kill . . ."
Paul English, *Oxford American*, January 13, 2015.

"I walked out of the studio . . ."
The Atlantic Sessions booklet, June 19, 2006.

"At the age of 39 . . ."
Review, *Rolling Stone*, August 30, 1973.

"I noticed that everyone dressed very comfortably . . ."
Guardian (UK), May 2015.

"We were determined to play our music . . ."
Larry King Live (CNN), April 16, 2010.

"I can't remember when a record has taken such a hold . . ."
Paul Nelson, *Rolling Stone*, August 28, 1975.

"This might be called a concept album . . ."
Review, *Billboard*, June 14, 1975.

"When this album came out I compared it . . ."
Review, *Rolling Stone*, 1977.

"It was a movement . . ."
Bill Ivey, *Baltimore Sun,* September 9, 1991.

"Record company executives are the worst at it . . ."
Guardian (UK), May 16, 2015.

"I had been wanting to do the album . . ."
Los Angeles Times, August 9, 2014.

"One of the reasons Willie had come to me . . ."
Booker T. Jones, Wonderingsound.com, May 11, 2011.

"In one sense, *Stardust* is a memory album . . ."
Review, *Rolling Stone*, July 1978.

"distinctive, soft vocal style to good use . . ."
Review, *Billboard*, July 1978.

"I loved the title outlaw though I don't think any of us were . . ." *Billboard*, June 2012.

"Trigger's like me . . ." *Texas Monthly*, December 2012.

"It has the tone that I like . . ." *Rolling Stone*, 2012.

"I had it taken out of the Baldwin . . ." *Frets*, 1984.

CHAPTER FOUR

"You haven't lived until you've heard Nelson stumble . . ."
Review, *Rolling Stone*, 1982.

"He leaned back and said, 'Who wrote this . . .?'"
Wayne Carson, Country Music Hall of Fame seminar, December 2011.

"I said, 'Well, I know I've been gone a lot . . .'"
Wayne Carson, *Los Angeles Times*, 1988.

"The Elvis version's beautiful . . ."
Ricky Gervais, *Desert Island Discs*, BBC radio, 2007.

"In 1982, they recorded *'Pancho and Lefty'* . . ."
Patrick Doyle, *Rolling Stone*, May 26, 2015.

"I loved Willie Nelson . . ."
Chips Moman, Georgiarhythm.com, November 2008.

"He said, 'No, I want you to come in here . . .'"
Merle Haggard, *Houston Press*, March 20.

"Death is not the ending of anything . . ."
Parade, June 2010.

"Leon came down to the first 4th of July picnic . . ."
Los Angeles Times, February 1996.

"He's a natural . . ."
Robert Redford, *Texas Monthly*, May 2008.

"Willie does it like a real person . . ."
Jerry Schatzberg, *People*, September 1980.

"It has its charms . . ."
Roger Ebert, *Chicago Sun Tribune*, July 1980.

"When I wrote the album . . ."
Chicago Sun Tribune, November 16, 1986.

"If you like the song, the violence is there . . ."
Life, August 1987.

"*Stagecoach* cracks its whip . . ."
Review, *Rolling Stone*, August 15, 2014.

"I'd hitchhiked around Texas . . ."
Steve Earle, talking to author, 1992.

"I was in London, finishing an album . . ."
Jimmy Webb, *Performing Songwriter*, August 15, 2012.

"Johnny was bigger than life . . ."
Mickey Raphael, AARP.com, April–May, 2016.

"It just sounded like something where it worked for everybody . . ." Johnny Cash, talking to author, 1988.

"We never had any problems . . ."
Waylon Jennings, *Music City News*, August 1985.

"Every one of these guys was my hero . . ."
Kris Kristofferson, *Weekend Edition* (NPR), February 3, 2013.

"Well we had all our families with us . . ."
Republican, May 12, 2010.

"I hope that some of the money . . ."
Bob Dylan on Live Aid, July 1985.

"The 1980s were a bleak time for family farmers . . ."
Editorial comment, *Modern Farmer*, August 24, 2015.

"In the 1980s, as I toured the country . . ."
Family Farmer, July 28, 2015.

"After I talked to Jim Thompson . . ."
Billboard, November 29, 2010.

"The concert was one of those moments . . ."
Rhonda Perry, *Time*, October 1, 2010.

"Farm Aid has raised more than $50 million . . ."
Farm Aid website (farmaid.org) 2012.

"Anyway, it's just about impossible . . ."
People, July 11, 1983.

"The whole thing—you know, it was such an unusual duet . . ."
Julio Iglesias, *Talk Oasis* (CNN) January 23, 2014.

CHAPTER FIVE

"I'm not easy to live with . . ." Parade.com, June 27, 2010

"She's been with me through thick and thin . . ." *Rolling Stone*, 2015.

"Was never spoiled when I was a kid . . ." Lukas Nelson, *Humboldt Beacon*, 2011.

"Well, I had invested in some tax shelters . . ." *Larry King Live* (CNN), April 16, 2010.

"He had more expenses going out . . ." Lana Nelson, *Texas Monthly*, May 1991.

"It's really nice that they want to do something . . ." *Entertainment Weekly*, November 30, 1990.

"It's no overproduced album with millions of dollars of studio costs . . ." *New York Times*, September 2, 1991.

"There are more serious problems in life than financial ones . . ." *New York Times*, September 2, 1991.

"Billy Nelson, the son of country singer Willie Nelson . . ." News item, Associated Press, December 1991.

"Willie was here in Nashville..." Willie Nelson management, December 1991.

"A guy like Willie and I . . ." Merle Haggard, Montereycountyweekly.com, February 2008.

"Bob Dylan was so knocked out . . ." Kris Kristofferson, *Billboard*, April 29, 2013.

"The title song was recorded in Dublin . . ." Don Was, *Detroit Free Press*, 1993.

"Obviously an important album for Willie Nelson . . ." Rick Mitchell, *Houston Chronicle*.

"Overshadowed in recent years by Garth-mania . . ." Review, *Entertainment Weekly*, April 2, 1993.

"The album's centre-piece . . ." Review, *Hot Press* (Ireland), June 1993.

"I really thought you had to die to get here . . ." CMA Awards, September 29, 1993.

"We found less than two ounces . . ." Police Sgt. Mike Cooper, *Associated Press*, May 1994.

"There was no cause to give me any problems . . ." *Entertainment Weekly*, September 1998.

"Here I was between labels . . ." *Billboard*, April 27, 1996.

"Her timing, while at first jarring . . ." Review, *No Depression*, October 1998.

"Spirit has certain similarities . . ." Chris Morriss, Trunkworthy.com.

"Ever true to his school . . ." Kris Kristofferson, 1996.

"Nelson's singing, with its craggy humanity . . ." David Fricke, *Rolling Stone*, December 13, 1996.

"I left it up to him, more or less, because . . ." *Stomp and Stammer*, April 1999.

"Gets the Daniel Lanois treatment . . ." Rob Sheffield, *Rolling Stone*, April 1998.

CHAPTER SIX

"The show belongs to Nelson . . ." Parke Puterbaugh, *Rolling Stone*, September 29, 2000.

"No matter how far afield the music takes him . . ." Review, *No Depression*, October 31, 2000.

"Nelson is capable of redeeming . . ." Review, *Slate*, March 4, 2005.

"Country music every now and then . . ." *Wall Street Journal*, November 11, 2001.

"I begged for it . . ." Luke Lewis, *Billboard*, December 17, 2001.

"Lost Highway has a great staff . . ." *Billboard*, December 17, 2001.

"Upon a casual listen . . ." Deborah Evans Price, *Billboard*, December 2001.

"I turned it over to Matt and let him run the whole show . . ." *Billboard*, 2002.

"Premier duet partner of all time . . ." Matt Serletic, OnlineAthens.com, February 2002.

"Someone told me the other day . . ." *Billboard*, 2001.

"A solitary co-songwriting credit . . ." John Aizelwood, *Guardian* (UK), June 2002.

"The troubled Spanish acoustic of the title song . . ." Review, *Rolling Stone*, 2002.

"I do what I feel like doing . . ." *Chicago Tribune*, 2005.

"Kris [Kristofferson] was telling them . . ." *Lonestar*, 2002.

"James and I, we had this formula . . ." *American Songwriter*, January 1, 2007.

"After more than five decades of recording . . ." Sue Keogh, BBC (UK).

"I started at the top . . ." Michael Hall, *Associated Press*, January 4, 2005.

"I drove the car . . ." *New York Times*, December 30, 2005.

"There is really no need going around . . ." Willie Nelson press release, 2006.

"I love him to death . . ." *American Songwriter*, January 1, 2007.

"Adams loves his band the Cardinals . . ." Robert Christgau, *Rolling Stone*, October 30, 2006.

"It was Luke . . ." *American Songwriter*, January 2007.

"Me and Merle . . ." Willie Nelson press announcement, April 2015.

"Lift the spirits . . ." Review, NPR radio, April 2015.

PICTURE CREDITS